How To WOW!!

Preface

Since I published *How to start a business without any money* in 2020, the same question has repeatedly cropped up: what business should I start?

While *How to start a business without any money* advised starting in whichever areas customers would spend money – ergo ascertaining their needs and desires – many readers asked me to be more specific regarding business model, online, service, and products.

So here it is – *What Business To Start*. Rather than lists and definitions based on my experience, the book is more of an operational overview.

1. Wander through a series of examples classified by type to understand better which specific business model would suit you and your customers.

2. Shape unique customer services with new business ideas.

3. Expect help with pricing.

4. Flex your abilities in ways that are both fun and worthwhile.

5. Learn to craft effective and practical solutions that deliver good value for money.

"David White has succinctly summarized the chief, simple but profound reasons businesspeople with ambitious intention, good ideas, and capability get 'de-railed' from their progressive realisation of success. David is of course, an experienced, successful entrepreneur and valued advisor to entrepreneurs, as well as a gifted teacher."

Dan S Kennedy, Author, Serial Entrepreneur, Strategic Advisor

"David's knowledge in business and marketing - hand in hand, with his unbridled energy and enthusiasm, inspires all to up their game. Always something to learn and improve - and always fresh ideas and angles — always pushing forward — and getting real results"

Lisa Catto, Consultant, and Coach

"It was my pleasure to connect with David on LinkedIn and have a call over skype. I learned so much. David shared many insights which I believe will be valuable in growing my business. He speaks and mentors from industry experience rather than cliches. Very refreshing and inspiring."

Christopher Collins, CTO

'David White is a powerhouse of the business invention. I've known him for about 6 years now and am always impressed by how he can take an idea and build it into something that can be used by a business. If you need any sort of new business strategy David is the man to go to. I have used his services many times and will again and again - his successes speak for themselves.'

Fergus McClelland CEO Vocaltrademark

'I met David at a business seminar and was immediately struck by not only his technical ability but also his business acumen. I have no hesitation in recommending David'

Craig Boddington, Managing Partner

Big thanks to Caroline Hurry, sub-editor who was superb, fun to work with too.

Also a shout-out to all the reviewers who leave reviews for books they enjoy. Without you it would be harder for others to find the good books.

If you think this is a good book, please leave a review. Thank you.

If you would like to give feedback on the book to the author send a message via Twitter to @tribalideas - please mention the book name

Please subscribe to the authors weekly newsletter here:
https://theauthorityfigure.substack.com/

Free 'How to WOW' video training available from the accompanying website:
Https://TheAuthorityFigure.com

Contents

Foreword

Hello, author David White here. I have spent decades in business, writing, and public speaking – all part of a successful model in my experience.

I mention my writing credentials for two reasons. First, if any bloopers have found their way past me and my editor, please forgive me and tell me so I can fix the manuscript. Secondly, this book is 100% about paying it forward. I received no payment to write it at all.

I willingly invested my time on the basis that some good may come from it. I have no specific expectations. I have found it a good business practice to start by helping others; if some want to reciprocate, they make themselves known. It is a game of chance, but I cannot tell you how many times it has paid off. So, I wait with bated breath!

I have run successful businesses since my early 20s. I went from an electronics apprentice to a freelance electronics engineer and from a project manager to a web consultant. I set up Weboptimiser, one of the world's first digital marketing agencies, picking up major brand clients from Adobe to Regents Park Zoo.

A diverse business, Weboptimiser ran for about 15 years during the search engine's rise. Pretty much BG (Before Google), which ultimately bought my business out.

I managed to head up the UK and EU Search Council for the IAB (where we defined the standard size of the banner ad) and even spent a day one-to-one with former Prime Minister Gordon Brown. Sky TV interviewed me about that day – perhaps hoping I'd dish some dirt. I didn't.

My day spent with our PM was between us. We didn't discuss politics. He was good to talk to and reasonably answered my questions.

I've enjoyed First Class flying and big cars, but I see no need to travel overseas these days. I rent a car to do business when I need one. Gone are insurance or parking worries. I had all that when I was younger. Now my companies are more eco-friendly, offering lower overheads and higher profits, I live a better life.

So, this book doesn't tell you what business to try so much as to supply you with greater awareness so you can ultimately make more informed choices.

This way, when you sit down and listen to a prospective customer, you will be more likely to craft an appropriate, creative solution to deliver with joy at an excellent price.

The better you can fulfil a customer's need, the more likely (although there is never a guarantee) the client will prefer to do business with you over anyone else.

In many ways having a customer preferring to do business with you over anyone else is the hidden advantage of the knowledge you will pick up, confirm, or clarify from these pages.

Please register at https://theauthorityfigure.com which is where you'll find some master strategies suitable for all entrepreneurs at any level.

Chapter 1: Where to start

Select a business based on who you are, where you have been and what you enjoy the most.

There are many reasons to set up a business and the first question to ask is what business to start.

The answer depends on who you are, where you have been, and what you want to do.

It is a good question to ask, the ramifications can be deep. If you get it wrong, it could mean your world may just fall apart. This is usually because we all have a different understanding of what a business is. Get it right, you could become a millionaire.

For some, running a business is a rite of passage. It is expected that one would become a captain of industry. For others, running a business is a vocation, a desire. For the rest of us, it is simply a means to an end.

Indeed, running the show is an instant promotion straight to CEO and it is a place where you have complete control. With the added bonus, you get to make all the profits. However, on the downside, if it goes wrong, you get to lose all the losses.

The simple way to avoid losses is not to invest or spend more than you can afford and, ideally, to maximize profits, spend nothing.

Why is this the ultimate guide?

First, this is a guide written by a practicing entrepreneur who has set up many businesses over the years and considered and rejected many more and started a few good successful businesses himself.

Second, you will find different business types, categorisations, benefits, and potential pitfalls to avoid, all to help you navigate different business opportunities. Plus, you will find useful information about incorporation, managing risk, and, ultimately, getting paid.

There are a few other books out there, most of which are about how to set up specific businesses. How to set up a roadside café, how to set up a truck business, how to invest and profit from a franchise and so on. These all appear to be perfectly good business books, just they are limited and focused, perhaps ideal if you know you want to start one of those businesses.

By virtue of the focused nature of those kinds of books, they cannot be the ultimate guide to knowing the best business to start.

There are other books that are clearly written by those who have very obviously never run a business. I am sure they are full of smart ideas, but, of course, missing actual experience. Again, due to limitations, while no doubt helpful to some, these books are guides perhaps, but they cannot be considered an ultimate guide as so much is missing.

I met a fellow author, George Haylings, very late in his life, in the US. He wrote the very popular and entertaining Discovered, 505 Odd Enterprises. It is a giggle of a book. He used to sell his books by mail order in the early days of print. The ideas are wild and range from providing dog food, to renting magazines to renting the roof top of your office as a sun lounger and, well, there are 502 more odd and unusual enterprising ideas within.

George's book is full of great ideas, although again it becomes apparent the book is full of suggestions and reports, not necessarily worked through businesses the author has experience of.

I come to this having been in business and having either operated or worked with, mentored and consulted those operating a wide range of different types of businesses. Practical experience, from the real world, built up over decades.

Any of these aforementioned books may well inspire you. If they inspire just one person to be motivated to start a business, then this can only be a good thing and certainly something I support. Financial independence and the freedom that comes from running your own business is worth it.

However, this book is the ultimate guide, I believe, the only ultimate guide, written by an actual entrepreneur.

This author has started up with his own money (and lack of it), against the odds, and had to make real entrepreneurial and personal decisions to start a business and keep it going, two important distinctions. You can only keep a business going if you first have a business to keep going.

As a result, you will discover real options and opportunities. You will understand more about what is involved, the downsides, the pitfalls, and the incredible opportunities. These are just some of what will make this book your ultimate guide to determining the best business to start.

3 types of businesses you should be aware of

There are 3 main types of businesses, the Passive, Service and Products businesses.

However, I have included a chapter on running an online business separately, which can be passive, service, product based, or a combination of all.

Invariably, you will start in one way, with one type of business. View the others as expansion opportunities, additional income streams ready to be tapped. Usually, quick and easy add-ons.

The most important objective of your business is to make money.

Therefore, considering different income stream opportunities is always a worthy subject and will help to protect your business. Don't get caught in the one area of business trap, as many do and get caught when it is too late.

Small and new businesses are fragile, so the quicker you can diversify into different but related markets and income streams, the more resilient, and more fun, your business will be. When you work a little harder, you will ultimately get paid more too.

It is important to understand that it is possible to run all three types of business simultaneously. It is the medium that typically changes.

Some customers want to be supplied with how-to information, some want to hire you to do the work for them, others may want to employ the tools you can supply and others like to help themselves through self-service (usually online) systems.

Understandably, some businesses will be more able to diversify than others.

As ever, the challenge is not to think an opportunity is impossible, but instead to rise to the challenge and to work out how to make it possible and put it to work.

I have run all three and am currently.

The more income streams you have not only provide a larger income, More income streams provide security, as if one should fail, then the others would likely remain.

A key business concept that many fall foul of is to put all your eggs into one basket. If your business fails, all is lost. With a more diverse business, if one income source stutters, trips or fails, then at least for a while, the other(s) may continue.

A passive business example

Writing books and selling them via Amazon is an example of a passive business I run. On a good day it can make money, having multiple books means the monthly income alone is not insubstantial, although it can take a while to build up. Being passive also means you have little control.

Having multiple books is an example of diversification.

Taking the books and publishing an audio version is another example of diversification.

It is also possible to sell the books through other publishers, not just Amazon.

It is best to decide to write a book, once you are certain there will be demand for it, on a topic you would feel comfortable with. Ideally, you have experience and an interest in the topic.

An easy, self-publishing, no cost model is to write the book, have the cover designed, lay it out and upload it to your distributor of choice. Your distributor then makes it available to retailers who stock and sell it.

Essentially, once the book is written, laid out and the cover is designed and uploaded, you are one and done. That is why a book is a passive business.

There is nothing to stop you from reviewing your work and updating it from time to time. It remains passive.

The distributors promote it to the public and through their bookstores. If the bookstores have customers interested in your type of book, they will be sold and the retailer will buy some more from the distributor.

The retailer and distributor make a small profit on each sale. Everyone in the chain gets paid, including the writer and publisher. You are the writer and the publisher. You set the price, this includes the opportunity to set a free price in order to give your book away.

You don't have to write a book to have a passive income, there are hundreds of options, vending machines, for example.

There are many more passive business opportunities listed in the Starting a passive business, chapter 10.

A service business example

A service business is where you provide a service, for example a cleaning service, and you return on a regular basis to clean an office, a kitchen, car, house or hotel. There are many things that require cleaning on an occasional or regular basis.

Often, you will provide your service to the same customer on a regular basis.

I have run a number of service businesses, and sometimes I put teams together for consulting projects. Other times, I provide mentoring and coaching services.

There is a long list of services you could provide, online it could involve writing code for machine learning, estimating, forecasting, data display or web scraping applications for comparative pricing applications.

As you are probably aware, service businesses exist in just about every sector, from high technology to car cleaning.

The objective, as always, is to think about what service you would like to provide and where the audience is for it and to determine a close match between your offer and their needs.

The beauty of most service businesses is that they require little by way of capital and are often very scalable and can be very cash-generative.

A product business example

Most product businesses involve the processing of raw materials to create a finished product.

This kind of business is normally engaged in the haulage, storage, processing, or manufacturing of goods. It often requires significant capital as space is usually required to store materials and you may need to buy materials too.

You can still run a lean business that minimizes your capital requirements if it is possible to acquire raw ingredients very cheaply or if you are able to buy them on demand and, in effect, have the customer pay for them. The dream is to buy only what you need when you need it and to use customers' money to do so (see chapter 15: Limiting liability before you use customers' money to do anything).

It is possible to take a range of services, bundle them together and refer to them as a product. One product I have is called the Authority Figure. It is actually a website, but there I have put together a series of materials and processes anyone can adapt and follow to become an authority figure in their market, more on this topic on the site and in chapter 13: Being the authority figure.

At a glance, when you visit the website, you will see 'How to Wow' offers. These are core products, site members get free access, and they are there to help members attract clients on an ongoing basis. Visit https://TheAuthorityFigure.com

The purpose of a business is to profit

It is possible to not spend a bean generating sales and make a profit.

It takes a lot of self-control. There are voices in our heads, who tell us to buy things. Buying is easy. Instead, we must find products or services for customers to buy.

Many come up with a bright idea about how to start a business that will succeed because it is different from that which already exists. It may be faster, bigger, brighter, taste better, be less expensive and so on, any number of things or all of the above.

These are great intentions and normally come at a price. Knowing this, many set about raising capital to fund and research a brilliant idea. I suggest you really don't focus on raising capital, instead focus on raising customers, they have money too.

There are untold numbers of business plans that have powered through to presentation and taken years to development just to raise no money at all. Of those that do manage to raise the cash they require, few have managed to succeed. I suggest you target success at the beginning of the process, not the end.

In other words, find a customer first. Raise money afterwards.

Once you have customers, raising money becomes super easy and you don't have to give away equity.

Your idea, whatever it is, will not be the same idea customers will buy.

An idea is like having a plan for war, and it falls apart on contact with the enemy. We want to avoid that, instead welcome and expect change.

How to solve the key constraints of business growth

The key constraint of any business is always finding the best way to satisfy customer needs.

What does a customer want?

What are they prepared to pay for?

You need to know the answers sooner, not later. Plus, once you have found one thing they will buy, what else can you supply would they also buy?

You can make a more comfortable car, but is it something people want to buy?

Do customers want comfort, or do they want lower costs or to move away from fossil fuels?

Do they want a car at all?

If all they want to get is from A-B, why limit them to a car, why not supply transport, whatever it is, to suit them at the time of need?

In this example, you would not need to set up a car factory and invest in design, instead you could find someone who has the means for transport and act as a middleman and supply the customer with what they want when they want it.

Once this is a proven idea and you can demonstrate demand, then you can look at raising money to finance a proven venture. In this way, you will likely give little to no equity away and get all the funding you need.

Every day, banks offer services that are 100% dedicated to sales financing. You can always acquire funds when you can demonstrate sales.

With sufficient sales, you can invest in the most plush offices you would ever want.

Interestingly, having run a business for decades, the people who mostly wanted to come on-site were the authorities to check the operated according to health and safety standards. Or it was the local council or the tax-man, we certainly do not want to look plush to them. Very few customers visited.

For those customers who did visit, you can always hire a meeting room by the hour, no one needs to know and local restaurants and bars are often ideal for most meetings, particularly if you want to maintain a friendly atmosphere.

Meet your customers on-site

Most customers will want you to go to them, as it is more convenient for them.

Even if you have a show room, many first meetings are best held at their site. You can meet with their team or family where it is much easier to understand their needs and work out how to best help them.

This is an example of using your customers' capital and investment. Let them pay for the offices they need and if you can use them at no cost, go right ahead. You can sometimes make arrangements when on site to meet with other non-related customers, and use, with permission, a customer office and meeting room to meet another customer.

It can make for a pleasant experience for your visitor and save travelling time and room hire too. It is cheeky, very agreeable, and proves how 'connected' you are.

Slash your business costs

There are many businesses that on the surface require a huge amount of finance to run, it can be off putting, instead treat it as a challenge.

Consider the restaurant business, you might not know, but the restaurant business is one of those businesses most likely to fail.

Most start with a location, take on a long-term lease or buy a property and take on a mortgage. Either way, the costs are high and often similar. Leaseholders may as well buy. However, I appreciate this may require funds you do not have to start with. In which case, switch as soon as you can afford to, but not for depreciating assets. The next step is to fit it out. This takes time and the costs are easily in thousands, often tens of thousands. For many, owning fulfils a dream and is started as a result of a pension pay out or inheritance. Decoration, style, signage, kitchen equipment, front of house tables and chairs, lighting, plants and uniforms, there is a lot to buy.

The money is quickly spent and once everything is installed to perfection, the services switched on, and you have paid for a complete fit and design, now you need to attract customers and still buy food. What if there are not enough? This is the problem most face. It then dawns on the owners that the business is a money pit. All the costs are lost and the lease and local rates will need to be paid monthly for what may be years. A disaster. A common one.

I don't want to put you off the idea of running your own restaurant one day.

Cut an idea down to size and test!

A restaurant is a worthy business, and we need good ones. It is just there are other ways you could start that could avoid the many costs involved. You may not like my suggestions, but many have and by not investing you can avoid the money pit completely and still take the idea of your ideal restaurant, cut it down to size and test it, then test it again and again.

The more you test, the better you will find your idea of a restaurant will work.

When you have a proven concept, one that satisfies actual customers and some of them recommend you, come back or ask for more, you know you are onto a winning formula.

You can find kitchens to hire that are either underused, or available at economic rates. These are the kind of kitchens food delivery specialists employ. They don't need a splendid location, and their business model is not based on passing traffic.

Then there are the chefs who travel to customers' homes and cook in their kitchens.

This can be big money and requires zero overhead, just marketing. Word-of-mouth marketing is free if you are energetic with your conversations.

Two ways you can become a restaurateur without exposure to risk and in a way where you can start finding customers first, not last.

Later, when your business is running, you can invest your profits if you want to pay for your own kitchen or to invest in a show restaurant, by then you may well find you have a large enough network.

You will probably find a range of cash-generating ideas that work, all of which can be pooled to pay for the increased overhead. However, may wonder why? If you have a perfectly good business, achieved while avoiding investment, why invest at all?

All businesses, to succeed, have to make a profit.

Profits will always pay for the lifestyle you want to live.

The question is: what kind of business to start?

I suggest that the answer is a business designed to succeed.

Coming up with an idea is one thing, implementing it is another. We have covered both to some extent, but what if you cannot come up with an idea? Or how would you come up with an idea if you don't already have one?

Well, this book was written to help you find your idea. We will cover some of the situations to consider before you start to make sure your risks are minimized. Few of us have money we can afford to lose.

It is time to become the B.O.S.S.

What you need to establish to create a business is a Business Operating System for Sales

Running a business is not about operations or development, it is about finding customers to sell to and then developing more and more solutions to meet their needs. This way, only a few customers may be required to earn a lot of money.

If you don't develop new things to sell or if your operations and deliverables are poor, or just generate very little profit, then you will go mad trying to find the many customers you need to make a business worthwhile. You may have heard the term busy fool, this is to be avoided and many businesses wear themselves out chasing after customers, selling each one very little.

Big companies have done this and they can bury losses, and play accounting tricks to hide poor results just to push them into next year and so on, yet what is really required is a solid business with a solid sales system. Client needs are the number one thing to focus on.

When you can sell a range of related items to a single customer, the cost of sale as a percentage diminishes greatly. Put another way, this means you can spend more time researching and finding how to 'buy' new customers, because you know when you find one it will be very worthwhile.

There are many companies who lead with a low cost offer, one that is irresistible and you may wonder how they make money, the answer is in all the other things that are sold to the customer, happily as a result.

Chapter 2: Common start-up myths - resolved

How to make sure you don't get lost chasing down blind rabbit holes.

I decided to set up my first business when I was very young and employed.

I had no idea, yet every preconception you can think of. I wasted a lot of time.

My father was in the accounting profession and suggested it would be a good idea for me to go see an accountant. He set up a meeting for me to meet another firm as he said that way he would have no influence and I could find out for myself what it was all about.

They were obviously a big outfit, and they had very nice offices. I was treated well and given lots of tea, biscuits and fatherly advice.

Years later, I remember concluding just two things. First, that was the kind of firm who would be great to have as a client, clearly they had a lot of money. Secondly, there was no way I would hire them as they would be way above my pay grade.

The good news was that, despite them doing their level best to put me off becoming an entrepreneur, I did manage to create several multi-million pound businesses without their help.

Myth #1 You need a business plan

The first thing I learned from the accountants was that I urgently needed a business plan.

The accountants detailed what it should contain and why. It was very interesting. The reason why I would want a business plan because, in their eyes, to start a business I would need to borrow some money.

I would accept you do need to do some research. You want to know as much as you can about the market and the lives and interests of your potential customers. Take notes, write them up, if you have time, write a book, and certainly read a few, they will be out there.

You will find either books that are golden nuggets, or, in most cases, you will find out-of date information. If this is the case, both are good news.

If there is great content, most of your competitors will never have read it. If there is rubbish content, there is an opening for you to enter the stage. Quite an opportunity.

If you find some new and useful books, read them carefully and try to adapt their suggestions to fit what you know and look for gaps in their knowledge, you may end up writing the ultimate guide.

You don't have to write a book, but if you are doing research it is not a stretch to take notes, to catalogue a little of what you find and from there, just write 3000 words for 15 days and you will have a book. Being able to point to a book and prove you are the author is a very respectable sales tool to use as a business card.

Funnily enough, banks like to work with experts...

The most important thing you can do, and I will repeat this, is to start.

Even if you start with the research.

Starting with research is not procrastination. Unless you really do know all you need to know and you have a client lined up, Research will pay dividends as it will help you find potential clients, it will likely provide you with factual certainty and confidence.

If you do have clients already lined up, you have got the most important elements already in hand. Note, research is never wasted even if it confirms what you already know and nothing more.

Myth #2 You need to borrow money

The last thing I wanted to do was to borrow money.

I was already dead set against that idea. I figured if I was able to get a loan, everyone would be into my business and I would never be able to get them out. I would be hounded to the edge of the world and back. They would be watching every move. I might even have to deal with industrial spies!

In any case, I could neither write a business plan for borrowing money as I really did not know what business I would be in. Strangely, no one had asked, or if they did, I would mention something about electronics services, as I was at the time, an electronics engineering apprentice.

You don't need lots of money to start a business. You do need what I call WAM - Walking Around Money.

WAM is money to pay for lunch and cover small expenses like the cost of buying a few books, transport, perhaps buying a smart suit if appropriate. Paying the bills while your business starts.

Looking the part is very helpful if you can follow through with some conversation and demonstrate knowledge and willingness to help. Chances are you will go a long way.

You do not need the very best, industry-leading equipment to get started either. The trick is to make a very small amount of money go a long way, once you have earned some money, you can spend it like a drunken sailor. That's your business. The only person you need to impress is yourself. Until then, you need to tread very carefully and string out what you have available, to keep the dream alive.

Restrictions breed creativity!

Myth #3 Perfection is everything

There is a term I love and it is minimum viable product, it is an agile project management term.

The idea is simply to prove a concept. It can be ragged, it can be incomplete, it can also be fast. If it works, it can be demonstrated and customers accept caveats provided they can see an operational outcome and its potential. This allows customers to tell you more about what they want and, as a result, they get a customised solution, made for them.

Yo get a case study and a customer.

You simply tell potential customers you can show them a proof of concept and go prove something to them.

In the past, I have created interactive demonstrations using nothing more than PowerPoint. It is easy to do. The focus was not on design in terms of look and feel, and the focus was on achieving a functional outcome.

Feedback from actual customers will allow you to reinforce or re-engineer the product for improvement.

The idea is to constantly ship, but continue to change and update the fabrication as you go. This way, there are fewer delays and you get paid to carry on innovating to your hearts content.

Myth #4 You need experience

You gain experience by doing stuff, chances are you have all the experience you need.

In truth, experience gives you a heading, a direction. Only when you get to your destination can you determine what to do next. Experience will certainly help, however, invariably at the destination, all the pieces are there, ready for you to assemble and, as a result, a positive experience.

It is possible to go into a client meeting and to be overtaken by the wishes and sounds of the client who then decides to give you a tour. You don't need experience to patiently listen. At the end, your potential client may then turn around having shown you everything and ask simply, well, can you do it?

The salesman should help you say yes, or in a worse case scenario, probably. Obviously, the more affirmative, the more likely you will get the business. Remember the potential client has already made up their mind you will be doing it, that is why they have spoken with you and given you a tour, to make sure they have shared all their experience so you know what is involved.

That is, great news, knowledge, and experience can be transferred.

Experience is invariably the ability to consume information like a sponge.

The main skill: you need to be a good listener!

Most waste years trying to accumulate more and more experience, just in case, when early on, they had all that was needed to find a way. At the end of the day, if you do get stuck, it is always better to ask a question and in most technical areas, someone else with experience is often made available to handle queries or follow progress, so there can be opportunity for discussion.

Another take on experience is to see it as an ability to problem-solve. Consistent learning is a key habit, having a library of resources and access to consultants or mentors, will help you find the answers when you need them.

We are all green when we start out. Everyone has to start from some where.

I started in business and took on some crazy responsibilities in my early twenties. No experience required for stupidity, yet despite myself, being mainly self-inflicted, it all worked out in the end. I survived to tell the tale.

The whole of life should be full of experience, preferably transformational ones.

Have fun.

Myth #5 You need an office, or a shop or a restaurant etc.

Millions of business owners use suites of free offices spread across the globe, they are at local coffee shops, diners, restaurants and, in the UK, some refer to them as greasy spoons.

I know someone who loved the food from a certain van vendor who always used to set up on the same road lay-by. He even had team meetings for his field reps there, no one had a problem parking and everyone got a hot mug of their favorite beverage.

In most cases, what you really need is a laptop, many go to work armed only with a mobile phone and a pair of scissors, some with even less.

Chances are when you start out you will be working alone and most likely travel to customer sites. Nowadays, you may find yourself working with a small fledgling founding team, chances are everyone will be a remote worker, working from home.

You only need an office if you have to have storage. Perhaps you run a distribution business and you have a yard, then an office would keep you warm and give you cover on rainy days.

In conclusion

The point here is not to say don't write a business plan, don't borrow money, don't seek perfection, don't get experience or avoid renting an office shop or restaurant.

It is to point out these things are not pre-requisites. By all means write notes and try to articulate what your business is about. Just that when you start out, most people don't know what they are going to do.

Like battle plans most business plans fall apart when they come into contact with a customer.

The only person who can answer the question of what is your business about is a customer who decides to pay you to do something. If you then decide you would like to do more of that work, that would be the time to write a business plan. Especially if you thought you could raise money as you able to demonstrate you have a great idea, because you have found a customer to willing to pay you for it.

The next question is can you get more customers without going broke.

Your customer may consider perfection is the whole point of hiring you, and you may believe you know how to deliver perfection at a cost that is profitable. Have at it!

The whole idea is simply this: avoid spending money. Find lower cost or free alternatives. As a new business owner you need to focus first and foremost on building up a cash reserve.

How To WoW!!

Chapter 3: What kind of entrepreneur are you?

Knowing yourself and potential customers personal interests can make all the difference.

Eight entrepreneurial types

Which of the following archetypes resonate most with you?

1: The Escape Artist

You have a job or career in the corporate hierarchy, yet recognize it is time to move on.

You might be a Dilbert fan and agree with much of the irony. You disagree with the unnecessary politics of work and would like to quit and do something more meaningful with your life.

You may play it safe and build something on the side, prepare to take early retirement, invest in a side hustle, or support a partner with their leap to freedom. Chances are you will wait for something solid.

When you are ready, you move with certainty.

2: The Diva

You know you deserve a high-flying lifestyle.

You are probably in a hurry to have the champagne, the wardrobe, the travel, and the lifestyle.

Strong on self-belief, you won't mind burning a few bridges and making a statement to succeed.

Ultimately, you seek a platform you can use as a stage. You relish recognition and acknowledgment. You want people to know who you are and to like you.

You dress with style and frequent the best restaurants.

Your high-flying celebration of life is visible to all.

3: The Designer

Your core motivators are freedom and flexibility.

You want to live your best life and work on the best projects with the best people. Your objective is to maximize the opportunities so you can mix pleasure with as little business as possible.

We are talking about lifestyles. You want to stay fit and take in life in all its many forms, work included, to provide the means to make it sustainable.

Chances are you will be very interested in passive and online business models. Designers don't always enjoy working with the customary 9 -5.

Chances are you will make a diverse range of models work for you and provide you with the ideal lifestyle.

4:The Provider

Your family is your top priority.

Nothing else comes close.

You know if your family are OK, you will be too. You don't have to fit in; you will make things happen to ensure everyone gets what they want.

If you notice layoffs coming., you will use the time to put things into place. You know how vital it is to maintain your income level with as much certainty as possible.

If all goes well, you could earn more than your dreams, so rather than see this as a downer, you positively meet your responsibilities in a head-on challenge.

5: The Enabler

Determined to improve the world, you know how to get things done.

You pro-actively find solutions to problems because your overall objective is to help others. Doing so will mean they will be around to help you.

You let others know you are a reliable resource, always ready for conversation and action.

You can set yourself up as a problem-solving service provider available on a short-term or ongoing basis.

6: The Prodigy

You thrive in careers that offer unlimited potential and don't hold you back.

Your boundless energy and enthusiasm drive you forward to get everything done well.

You hate constraints. Since most employers have difficulty pinning you down, you succeed best by being the boss or an inspirational leader.

You set and achieve goals. You deliver on big dreams and thrive on big projects, working with influential people.

It is time to start building your empire. Hi ho!

7: The Potter

As an experimenter, you will try something 1000 times. You love working by yourself to achieve great things. Better still, if someone pays you for it.

The politics and waiting around involved in teamwork frustrates you. Working solo, you can crack on, identify and solve problems as they arrive. The important thing is to focus on one project at a time, not get side-tracked or start spinning a series of items or wander off in search of something interesting.

Get some cash results, then move on to the next area of activity. Ensure you leave time to check previous operations are still working.

You will likely value leading a team delegating so you can move on to the next project again.

8: The Artist

You love the process of creation and the dopamine hit of recognition it brings.

It keeps you craving for the next project, so you need tight discipline to create repeatable processes rather than exquisite, potentially-costly one-offs.

You share some of the traits of the Potter and the Designer; therefore, passive, hands-off businesses will appeal to most.

Separate your art from the business, or work at creating systematic processes to enable the sourcing of new clients and fresh pieces to sell.

Which are you?

You are undoubtedly unique, yet one of these archetypes should appeal more than the others to help you clear up ambiguity. Discovering your personal 'why' helps nail down your focus so that you can more confidently resonate with your target audience, making the sales process more accessible.

Being transparent about who you are and what motivates you is no bad thing. Most find honesty an admirable quality. A common trait of a good salesperson is a chameleon-like ability to blend in with people and make it seem like you are one of them.

On this theme, the more you know about characters and archetypes, the more you can adjust your approach toward potential customers and give them what they want.

Understanding your nature and circumstances related to each archetype can motivate you to succeed even when customers say no, or go broke. Life happens.

Inner strength is vital. Knowing who you are and clarifying why you do things help.

Chapter 4: The 2 principal customer strategies

Pivot when you can and find more items to sell.

When it comes to deciding what business to start, most of us look at our experience, qualifications and successes.

We might feel we know the kind of services customers need and we know how to deliver it to them.

Two sides of the coin

If one side of the coin is our experience, the other side of the coin is all about the potential needs of our clients. The bigger picture side of the coin is the potential needs. This will lead you to even more opportunities than you may realise.

Perhaps for whatever reason, we have no experience, or perhaps the last thing we want to do is to do more of what we have been doing. Perhaps the objective is to get out of a rut, to seek change, to do something different, to escape from our current existence? In which case, more of the same is the last thing we want.

Of course, following a passion is a good thing to do if you can, not everyone has that opportunity. Some may prefer a change.

Whichever side of the coin you consider, you need to discover exactly where the opportunity lies for you. This is not as difficult as it may seem. Even if you are not sure what to do.

Just because you do not know what to do, does not mean there is nothing to do. Conversely, you may think you know what to do, yet the market could be too limited and ultimately too small to generate a consistent and growing income from just one service or product area.

There is a whole world out there.

The simple answer is to talk to customers and find out what they want.

Who is a customer? Everybody!

Everybody is a customer of someone. No one has to be your customer. You can find customers of other suppliers and simply talk to them about their purchases, what they were looking for, whether they got what they were looking for, more, or less. The more we know, the better.

We want to know the things that delight and we want to know where pain exists too.

We all need to eat, drink, exercise, and sleep. So we need food, nutrition, exercise, a bed and so on. This is basic, yet in simple terms, this is where it all starts, we need to know what others want so we can deliver it to them.

You are looking for more than simply a way to decide what you can do. You must find a problem customers are willing to pay to solve.

Early lessons

When I was a teenager, unable to drive, without income and with no possessions, the same as every other teenager, I could see my neighbors had cars.

It made sense to me to ask those neighbors if they would like their cars cleaned and if I were to clean them would they pay me. Most said they did not need their cars cleaned and would not pay me. I thanked them, moved on and asked the householder of the next house that had a car outside.

I kept asking and, after a while, a sufficient number of neighbors said they did want their car cleaned and they would pay. That was my first business. I stuck to my guns, and my main ability was perseverance. Of course, I had nothing better to do, it was a sunny day and it was fun to meet so many of the people who lived near me. Few took much interest in me, other than what I could do for them.

I had to walk some way to earn a decent amount. After my first day, I remember wondering what I might do with all the money I had earned.

No one put me up to it, I was not dared or cajoled.

It simply made sense to me to talk to the local householders who had cars and find those who might be prepared to pay someone to do it for them. A simple, straightforward mission. I found enough.

I remember some congratulating me for having the guts to knock on doors and ask for the business. They told me I had the makings of a businessman. It really did not seem a big deal to me. It seemed an obvious thing to do.

I got to clean some amazing collectors' cars too.

Little did I know how rich my neighborhood was.

I discovered negotiation, humour, bonus gifts, add-ons, cash collection and the importance of listening, keeping appointments, regularity and more.

I learned mechanically how to do the work.

I discovered and learned an incredible amount.

I had found a whole new world. It was all new to me.

Bear in mind, I had never cleaned a car before. I did not own one at the time.

It was an adventure.

Some of the owners even gave me their preferred cleaning equipment, so I learned from customers what customers wanted. It seemed reasonable, and, dare I say, professional, to go buy those cleaning materials for other customers.

All my customers were delighted to see my service improve and know that although it was just car cleaning, the service was improving and they were being taken seriously.

I was able to increase my prices.

Especially as now I had materials to pay for.

I learned the power of cheeky humor.

I would arrive and be congratulated for arriving on time, and told how much they wanted to support my little enterprise, which made them feel good. To which I would reply 'that's great, thank you, don't hang around, put the kettle on then!'

This way, I would get paid and get a drink for my troubles too. It was always taken in good humour and for some, I would clean windows, mow their lawn and take on other tasks, including helping them to move furniture or help clear their garage. Fond memories, halcyon days.

The point is, it does not matter how you start. Starting is key. Simply doing odd jobs for people can be very rewarding. I had a friend who would join me and we would go out together. While I developed a career in electronics, he stuck to it and became a partner in a household clearance firm.

Many of his customers were relatives of the elderly who had passed away and on occasion he would be offered the opportunity to buy the garage once it was cleared. Over the years he bought a few. Ostensibly for storage. Albeit each at a knock-down price. Now he is a property multiple millionaire and owns hundreds of garages.

Cleaning may not be the highest payer, yet it may be quite surprising where it leads to and back then, I did have some surprisingly good pay days. My old friend is delighted!

Those local householders for whom I cleaned cars were young, old, middle aged, male, female, professional, athletic, retired, ex army, or worked for the local council or ran their own businesses. I found, as a result, I was talking to just about everyone.

I quickly turned from a shy and introverted teenager with an interest in electronics, to an outgoing, talkative young man who loved nothing better than spending time outdoors in the sun making friends with the locals and drinking tea.

Some even had attractive daughters. But that is another story, for another type of book.

Inside opportunity

When we know an industry, chances are we have the skills to make a business of it.

We are likely to know what clients will need initially, next, and how to look after them over time. If you have it, and have enjoyed delivering it, this is very good inside information.

I always remember as a young electronics engineer how the project managers were always in trouble. They would agree with the boss, just to keep him happy.

The project managers would then slink back and quietly ask the team (or me) to quickly put something together to make it look like we had been working on the project for some time.

Clearly, skull duggery was afoot and it was not a very pleasant place to be, albeit mildly hilarious at the time. Understand this is the real world where the main game seems to catch up or get caught out.

You could not help but think there must be a better way.

Over time, the idea built that there is a better way.

After all, you are the one doing all the work, getting paid the least, yet taking all the risks. Plus, if things don't work out, or go wrong, you take the heat too!

After a while, you think it would be reasonable to cut out the middle man and go direct. However, it is not always easy.

My area of electronics at the time was missile guidance, so it was not like I could pick up and start up the next day as a missile guidance expert. No one would or could hire me and the chances would be high I would be arrested for potentially releasing state secrets.

By the way, that was decades ago and I have no recollection of what I was working on. In fact, most of us had no idea, no one, it seemed, had access to the detail, or even the big picture.

So for me and most people who would not want to compete with their former employer (as you never know if you may need or want to go back) you need to find a way to pivot.

Pivot when you can

Pivoting is where you take what you know and apply it in a different way to a different line of business.

For example, you could pivot from design to maintenance. In my case, I pivoted from missile guidance (radar) to consumer electronics.

Consumer electronics still require power, inputs and outputs, interfaces, software, there are many similar application areas.

I soon found myself as a contractor on a new portable computer design team, being paid nearly 10 times as much as I had when I was an apprentice. A great pivot.

I took what I knew and worked out how to offer it to a different audience and they bought it.

This was my first experience as a contractor. A short-term 1 month contract turned into a year and it allowed me to work on other things too. I could partly work from home (WFH), decades before WFH was an accepted term.

Contracting is not the only option available to you. However, it is a good one, as it does not require much more than you already have, if you have them: skills and knowledge based on experience. Plus, it gives you access, as I discovered, to big money.

A contractor does not need to invest in any equipment or offices or cars or photocopiers or make any long-term financial commitments.

You operate similar to an employee, you turn up, or work from home.

It is generally a wise idea to find more than one customer to ensure continuity and to maximize income. I have heard some contractors run 3 to 4 contracts all at once. That must be confusing yet attract an enormous income if you can pull it off!

The chances are you will have some of your own equipment or tools. A minimum of a laptop, for example.

Continuity of income

If you have the skills, and knowledge-based experience, then the next most important consideration before you start, is continuity of income.

There are plenty of other ways to go on your own.

Many aim to set up their own shop, embody the big dream and demonstrate to others you are serious about your plans.

The problem is that most of these business opportunities require some kind of medium term investment and there is a need to cover costs, this can become a substantial problem.

Many, having never set up in business before, will look to demonstrate some form of professionalism in advance. They might take on the rent of an office, have logo's designed, cards and stationary printed.

Why not? We are conditioned by TV programs and films which often show freelance detectives fired from the force, trying to take on cases and struggling to pay the rent, avoiding the landlord or landlady. It may seem comical, romantic even.

Yet it is incredibly serious, disasters can and do occur.

Discipline must be applied to ensure costs are avoided during start up and then only funded out of earned profits.

I would suggest renting only what you need when you need it. Try not to commission unique or original design work, because of the costs in terms of time and money required.

Instead, go on a search for potential customers first. Find out what customers need. Be honest, tell them you are starting up, which is why you don't have a card and have not sorted an office yet. I did this and my first client said I can use their office, they had the space and as I was willing to help them, they were delighted to help me. Free. Plus they were a design firm, so they did my design work for me to. Great people!

I have seen some hire expensive, exclusive addresses and take on long-term leases, for offices, equipment, cars, and in some cases, staff, all in anticipation of running a cracking business.

Their dream is to build it, and they will come. This often leads to disasters.

I have seen families wiped out due to their overly strong belief in their own potential success.

It is great to be and feel confident, just don't let yourself be tricked into making big cash outlays or commitments before you have cash income to cover the costs.

You will make mistakes.

Mistakes are part of the nature of being in business.

Mistakes are to be expected.

Customers make mistakes.

Orders get cancelled.

Deliveries go to the wrong addresses.

What you think you need, you generally end up not needing.

What you intend to sell, is often not what customers buy.

These are not gold rules, most of the time we get it right, yet so often what we think will happen happens with a variation, sufficient to render an original concept useless forcing you to embark on something else to pay bills and keep your best customers happy.

This is why it is best to find customers before you give up your job and pivot, before you invest in overhead. You will discover there is much you don't need.

So invest in equipment, design, cars etc., when you are ready, when your income is smooth and high, after an upward spike.

This upward income spike typically comes from established customers. This is why it is so important to focus on getting those first.

The most sensible of us will establish the security necessary to ensure continuity of income first and foremost. Only then will you decide how much you can afford to spend.

It is not a horse or cart question.

You don't need an office or equipment first.

What needs to come first is a customer and the accompanied ongoing income.

You can imagine success, but imagination does not pay bills.

Unless, of course, you are paid to imagine, and a lot of design work, including electronics design, is imagination, followed by development and testing.

These are things you can get paid for.

Chapter 5: The 2 most common ways to start a business

How to turn an passion or a frustration into a business.

There are many ways to start a business, most either turn a passion or a frustration into a business.

The passion business

A new book called Dice Men, written by Ian Livingstone, describes how and why he built a business now worth £2bn. Ian formed Games Workshop and developed Warhammer, a dungeons- and dragons style game with his friends. He built this business out of a shared passionate interest.

Interestingly, he notes that the banks would not touch him. He appears to be one of those who started a business with no money. Livingstone is to be congratulated for having recently been awarded a Knighthood as he was included in the New Year's Honours List.

My first business started at a similar time, albeit with less stellar results. Sadly, I have not been awarded a knighthood, but I have had fun. My first business lasted just three years and it was a passion that turned into a business. The issue was that I sold add-ons that only worked with a certain type of home computer and when that computer became less popular, as most products do eventually, the volume of the business tailed off. Eventually, the business was toast. I had to start again.

Indeed, I have started multiple businesses over the years. It is this experience of starting again I am able to draw from. Expecting change helps me continue to be in business today.

There are many passions. You can access lists and lists of them online. Plus, they feature in calendars. Search for hobby holidays, and you will quickly unearth sites that list hobbies and special interest days all year round. These are good to know, as they can help show you which hobbies are popular and the most relevant times of the year for them.

Many great businesses have been built around hobbies, such as Stamp Collecting, for instance, and the globally known philatelic brand and store: Stanley Gibbons. Apple created the now iconic iPhone and has cultivated a passionate following.

There are far cheaper cell phones available, but Apple has been able to combine the need to make a call by delivering a system that is easy and fun to use, that overcomes most of the frustrations many users have with similar equipment, and, as a result, is able to charge more too.

The frustration business

Most businesses are in the solving frustration business. Take a simple bread shop, for example. They sell a commodity product, one that is required by most people around the world on a daily basis, loafs of bread. They solved the problem of cooking a loaf of bread. They take the time, they have built big ovens and produce tons of bread on an industrial basis every day, so you don't have to. Instead, you just pop along to the store and buy bread along with all the other items that are made by others for you.

There are always new food ranges being developed. One of the more recent ones is all the ingredients for a curry, supplied in plastic pouches collated together into a single packet, all you need to do is to add the contents of the pouches to chicken to make a complex and tasty curry. It saves tons of time in preparation and delivers good food, too.

Vacation businesses provide an antidote to the frustrations of work.

The frustration business could well be the bigger business. Even though Stanley Gibbons serves hobbyists, the outfit also solves a problem as they are engaged in accessing rare and collectable stamps from across the world as a professional service.

Just about everyone and every market has frustrations, we all want more done, more quickly, for less. Normally we are looking for an answer to the question of what is the one thing you are most worried about or losing sleep over?

3 vital keys to success

Irecently published a Twitter thread on the 3 keys that unlock sales success and they are: to expect to change to adapt to customer needs, under-promise and over-deliver, and to spell things out for your customers as clarity is king.

These may each appear to be both a little mundane and obvious, yet many entrepreneurs do not employ these simple keys and instead make outrageous claims and stack 'em high, sell 'em cheap promotions to little effect, permanently self-forced to chase their tails.

However, here's the deal. At some point, usually sooner than later, your target customer will receive your goods and realise your goods are rubbish. You now have no chance of follow-through and future profit potential.

When we review Dice Men, we discover how players were fascinated by the game. The business started because so many people wanted to know how to play the game that Ian and friends started a newsletter to share ideas, updates and the 'rules' of the game, which one suspects were largely made up.

Yet this was fun, playing the game was the product, and it did not require a hard sell. The rules were changed to adapt to customer expectations, and there was not much of a promise, so it qualifies as an under-promise, which was: play the game, enjoy it, or not. Lastly, for clarity, the rules were written down, what started as a newsletter, became a guide and was developed into an income-generating magazine that continues today.

The 3 key Twitter thread:

3 vital keys to starting your next business

3 keys to unlocking success

Use them time and again

Save time and max sales

1/ All customers change and businesses adapt to their needs
Your suggestions are rarely what customers buy
Adaptation is the mother of necessity
The first key is to be open to change

2/ Under promise and over-deliver to wow with clarity
Tell customers what the deal is, why you want to help
The key is not to promise what you can't deliver
Be honest about what you can and can't do
Most clients will respect this
Honesty is the best policy

3/ When you achieve agreement, write it down and spell it out
Send a note to your customer in writing, an email is fine
You must cover what, when, and how much
You can attach a word or PDF with all details

If there are issues, better to iron them out beforehand
It is professional, to confirm your deal in writing
Each and every deal, particularly continuations
Avoid working twice and getting paid once

This may seem like common sense yet in the heat of the moment
Especially when it is your first customer, details can be lost
Changes in personnel lead to simple misunderstandings
Having it all spelled out reduces the chance of error
Enhance the chance of getting paid

You can outline other terms, such as the amount required upfront

Transfer of ownership, copyright, non-compete, not hiring staff

There are many terms to cover, basic terms, and conditions

None of this is difficult, yet it is imperative it is done

https://twitter.com/TribalIdeas

Chapter 6: What kind of business to avoid

Try to avoid the expensive kind!

If you have got the picture a business not to start is the expensive kind, you would be right!

If you have got the picture a business not to start is the expensive kind, you would be right!

Unless, of course, you had a lot of money to invest and you specifically wanted to create a capital-intensive business.

However, for most of us, the last thing we want to do is to deliberately take big risks for big money, especially if we have not got it, yet it is very easy to get into a high-risk, big money situation.

The worst combo: big money over time

I speak of personal experience, as I have made a few high-risk moves in my time and basically hoped for the best.

In hindsight, this was very foolish, naïve. Two involved the horrendous combination of time and money.

The first was when I set up a contract to buy 10,000 keyboards. Basically, I wanted the cost of development to be as close to nothing as possible (as I was in my early 20s and had nothing) so I agreed to place an order to buy 10,000 keyboards to spread and minimize development costs.

The truth was, I was not sure I could sell one.

You can see why this was a risky move.

Long story cut short, I sold 20,000 pieces over three years. Phew.

My second big self-enforced error was when I wanted a big office.

Without thinking it through, I signed a five-year lease.

At the time, it simply seemed to be the only way I could get the office of my dreams. I could afford monthly payments and this was cool for about two years. In the third year, I had to go without food on occasion.

To cut a long story short, I made it work in the end and sailed through years four and five. Close call.

Was it worth it? Well, yes, I was lucky. As many people said to me many times, I was young enough to recover.

Would I do it again? Absolutely not.

My conclusion: you should never employ luck as the basis for business strategy.

Looking into the future and hoping things will work out is a crazy idea.

Nowadays, I would look very closely at the minimum of everything and want to see a way out within a short term cash flow horizon.

In the case of the keyboards, I did not even have cash flow.

I simply had very strong beliefs. By the way, when the first keyboards arrived there was a big problem, they did not work.

The keyboards were to my design specification and I thought the problem must be a slapdash, self-enforced schoolboy error.

It took me two weeks of fretting and no sleep before it was found to be a build issue. It turned out there was a simple missing part, no one had thought to inform me.

I really had no idea what I was doing at the time.

I hope I most certainly will not do these things again. For every option, I routinely consider the amount at risk and the time period. I now know how to use a spreadsheet to work out how things look over time and life is calmer and much safer as a result.

With regard to space, the good news nowadays is that you can simply find the space you need when you need it. The commercial world has changed so there is simply no need to take on a 5 year lease.

Avoid solutions looking for problems

Many are known to have had a great idea and work tirelessly to perfect it.

These people are called inventors and over the years many have registered fantastic inventions that have never been made. As good as an invention might be, if the market does not have a problem to solve, why would they buy it?

Unfortunately, many people fall for this trap and work out how to get something done more quickly or efficiently, if there is no demand, then there is little chance of success.

My simple advice is to look for the problem first.

I know many authors who have written extremely nice, pleasing, articulate, and smart books who have great difficulty achieving sales. Every time I can see it is because the title of their book does not relate to a problem they are solving for a reader.

A friend wrote a book, its title was searched for, about 2,000 times. However, it did not solve a problem with the title. I have a book I wrote, well written if I say so myself, the title does not solve a problem, it says what it is, and the term is searched for. Both books are on page one of their respective terms. Few buy the book. Why, we are not clear on the problem we solve for the reader. Instead, we have a solution looking for a problem.

The problem is possible to fix.

It requires further research and the identification of a specific problem.

The key for your product or service business is to have people search and for you to appear as the best and preferably only solution to the problem.

Copyright may be worth registering

Technically, as an author, you do not have to register copyright as you automatically own it.

Again, I have registered certain inventions of my own. They have mainly been done to protect copyright, for example the copyright of this book.

However, by registering you will put a time stamp on your work. There are registries around the world, none of whom are required, the one I use is copyright.gov a US government department.

I figure if I was to have a dispute then the third party registration with a large internationally recognized government department will most likely be recognized. If nothing else, peace of mind for a relatively small cost.

An unexpected benefit is that it can be very easy to prove to media publishing companies who owns the copyright of your work.

First, find problems to solve

For all those businesses that start with a great idea where research or investment is required, you should first get a customer.

You may prefer to use the term sponsor, and some might perhaps prefer the term early investor. Whatever you want to call them, you are looking for someone who has a clear vested interest in your success. Someone who recognises the problem you say you can solve, who really wants that problem to be solved and is prepared to pay for it.

In effect, if all you have is an idea, it needs to be sold to prove it's value.

I would recommend even if you have the money, you should test your idea as early as possible to attract a partner or investor willing to back the idea from an early stage.

This helps to demonstrate that at least one other person sees merit in your idea, it is very important to identify a real customer need where customers exist who are willing to pay for a solution, or in the beginning, prepared to invest where the return is they will be the first to have the problem solved for them.

They, in turn, will become your case study and provide great insights into what they really want and become a willing partner and test-bed for you.

The consideration is always financial.

Someone has to be sufficiently impressed to put cash down.

We are talking about putting money where your mouth is. It is not sufficient for someone to say they will pay for it when they are ready, as the chances are they will not.

It is easy to say "I was keen to encourage you" you don't need encouragement, you need conviction. Conviction of the idea and approval of you as the supplier.

Perhaps you cannot find anyone to invest in and you are not keen or are unable to invest in yourself. In which case, you need to find an alternate method to start the business, one that does not require the level of finance you think is ideal.

Ultimately, you will need a customer and the sooner you find one, the sooner you can be certain you have an offer that could become commercially viable.

Also, with an actual customer, you will probably find a shorter way to deliver something that works. This could become a beta or an initial product or service that genuinely helps customers and drives cash into your business. There are many advantages to having a cash-generating business. One, of course, is being able to live and for a business to survive without selling equity. It will also mean, if you sell equity that the value of the equity will be higher because you do have a customer or customers.

Having more than one customer increases your safety net.

Every business I have started always started with an initial customer.

There is always a way

Someone, somewhere, already owns what you need or could provide you with access either for free or on a pay as you go basis, without a long-term contract for you to test.

It is Ok to test an idea and then to find out it does not work.

60

That is, the point of testing.

Your business idea may not be a complete failure. It may just fall in one important area.

It may prove impossible for you to produce, or you can produce but not sell, or you can produce and sell and yet, for some reason, the product or service is returned or rejected. The sooner you find out why, the better.

If, on the other hand, it is accepted, then you may have the green light to go sell some more.

As each problem is presented, your job becomes to know how to iron out the problem, to find a solution.

Every business starts with significant problems.

Usually, the biggest problem is finding a commercial need. Invariably, solutions are technical in nature, you may or may not have the technical knowledge required.

Can you acquire more knowledge and expertise in your area of enterprise? Can you find someone who does know? Can you persuade them to work for you? Can you cajole them to work for you for free?

Perhaps you can come up with a realistic profit share solution. Or, partner with an expert. There is nearly always someone, somewhere who will.

Regulated Industries

Regulated industries come with good and bad, the good news is generally a higher barrier to entry, to fewer competitors, the bad news is the higher barrier to entry!

However, it depends on who you know and what you know. You may be able to skirt around the barriers. I have a small cyber business, there are no IT solutions within, it is a framework and I provide training, it is designed for customers to think through the business in accordance with the architecture I have laid out for them to follow. This means I have no access to their secrets and we can discuss the approach without discussing their business at all.

I had to consult with the administrators of a UK-based weapons storage facility. I am led to understanding that it was the biggest in the UK. I do not know where. I do not know what. I do not even know the names of the people who attended the meeting. They all had name badges, although they told me when we started they were not their real names and whenever I mentioned a location or the weather or a region, they simply smiled.

Was it a set of nuclear bunkers - I don't know, was it for the navy, army, or air force, I have no idea. No one wore uniforms. All I do know is the location of where we met and some had to travel, or maybe all of them did. Again, I don't know, I can't be sure. I did not need to know how to deliver the training and show them how the system worked and how they could adapt it to their requirements. If you are interested in knowing more about my cybersecurity program, search for ESORMA on Amazon.

So certainly, in all countries, Military sectors are regulated, as are biological, medical and financial, to mention a few, there are more.

They can be problematic and yet these can also limit competition and single you out as being the only supplier for that sector. Being ideally accredited and known as the only supplier for a sector can be very powerful for making sales and could be considered positive. Many businesses are successful because of the very narrow focus they have on customers.

Specifically, choosing to target a regular industry may be an ideal approach and may help you define a business you can start few others would.

Capital Intensive Industries

Unless you have incredible access to capital, and are well trusted, capital-intensive businesses are likely to be prohibitive for most of us.

In many senses, this is common sense. If you need money to trade and you do not have it, you can't trade. Or can you?

I have worked for many finance companies who provide loans and mortgage services, it turned out it was not their money.

EXAMPLE: FX, investing, manufacturing, restaurant/retail, distribution

Service business: solar panel cleaning, baking, local delivery, roof repair, pool cleaning, car washing,

I was an agent for an agent, who, no doubt, in turn, was an agent of syndication. I did not have a relationship with the financier, I was able to cultivate relationships with potential customers.

The finance house only wanted to spend time working on approved, serious applications. The agency was there to drive the business, pre-qualify and get the applications completed and submitted in a complete form. It was my job to find people who were interested in getting a new mortgage on their property, prepared to take a call to discuss the possibility of completing an application (the form).

I love selling money.

All selling is really selling money.

In effect, you are saying to clients spend X to acquire Y, that includes X, so the customer always gets a return on investment. In its purest form, this is known as ROI, return on investment.

Anywhere you can spend a dollar and get more than a dollar back is a place that will generate more profits than simply putting your money in a bank and living off the interest.

You just have to make sure that when and if you enter a capital-intensive industry, that it is not your money at risk. For instance, in most forms of real estate, you are likely to either get paid for a service delivered or receive a commission as a percentage of the ultimate sale. For many, this is a very good business.

However, the more people that compete, the lower the commissions or fees you can levy.

The question of ethics

The question of ethics can be vexing, and depends on your moral view of the world and can extend to areas of ecology.

By ethics we could consider gambling, the sex industry or even renewables. We may be against gambling, sex, military, or animal testing and insistent whatever we do contribute to ecology and adds to our world in terms of renewables rather than adding to the ongoing destruction of our world and habitat.

In most cases, this is a simple choice and a valid consideration.

In many cases, it is a question of governance, although for all of us there are limitations concerning compliance. We have no choice but to comply with the law, and increasingly there are many laws about these topics, from the sex industry to gambling, to renewables, ecology and the reduction of emissions and responsibilities for security, health and safety.

There are industries you could enter, where you need to be aware of the constraints. Constraints can be the reason why you are suited to a given industry and you could find yourself running a business as one of the select few.

For many reasons, I chose not to work in the gambling, military and sex industries, partly for personal ethical reasons and partly as I want to play a constructive role in the world. Each to their own, these are my preferences.

I have lost business to those who do operate in those sectors and good luck to them. Equally, I have worked with customers who would not have wanted to work with me because my business supported anything they might consider unethical. So you win, or lose, both ways. I believe, on balance, ethical has a longer shelf life.

Also, when it comes to ecology and renewables, these are choices you make with suppliers. Some businesses decide to dedicate a proportion of sales or profits to supporting a charity or organization that fits with their views. When it comes to emissions, I choose to eliminate them along with waste, the best part, as Elon Musk likes to tell us, is no part.

Chapter 7: Start an online business

A modern website is more than an interactive business card - although that is pretty good place to start!

There are many ways to acquire the information you need, from publications, current practitioners, their customers, and other people who have similar problems to solve.

Any business can be an online business, it is a good idea to set up a website, as there are a number of useful practical applications you can get value from.

Get yourself a website!

The first piece of value is simply a place to make a statement about what you are about and to offer enough information so visitors can make contact or buy something.

You should try offering free information too, so you can start building a list of people who have registered an interest. Experience in making irresistible offers is vital for growth. You want to know what works and what does not as soon as possible.

Usually a how-to guide, or what to avoid when buying or investing in your kind of service, or a 5-steps to getting started, a checklist or free calculator or other tool may be the kind of thing most site owners offer.

Essentially, a website should provide some value to a visitor, collect an email address and then let you know when one has been collected so you can follow up.

If you are technically minded, you can set up an AWS account and buy your website address and configure hosting through them and then pay only for traffic, so if you happen to get no traffic, the site will cost nothing on an ongoing basis apart from the URL annual renewal fees which are likely to be roughly $15 U.S. per year. In any case, if you set up a brand new account at Amazon, currently the first year will be free anyway, as they encourage you to use their services. That is Amazon's irresistible offer.

Essential kit and connections

After that, you do not need a lot of money, although money can buy advertising.

You will need a laptop or desk computer, as powerful as you can afford and an internet connection. Once connected, set up a paypal and a stripe account so you can pay money and have more than one way to receive money. Also, open a Gmail account and get access to Google docs, which will provide a good amount of free cloud storage, access to spreadsheet, word processing software and more tools.

These are not difficult to arrange.

Software

There are a couple of tools to consider, the first already mentioned is Google Docs via GMail and the rest you will need to pay for if you want them.

If you are creative, you may want to invest in Adobe suite and you will get access to all the top-level creative graphics and video-making software you will ever need. Learn it once, and you will be able to make top-quality products.

A cheaper option is to sign up with an online service such as Canva, visit https://canva.com/ it is cheaper and not so professional, not that anyone would notice. You might want to upgrade later, maybe a year or two. In the short or medium term, if you are doing everything yourself and want to minimize the lessons you need to learn, and time is an issue for most of us, Canva is great and with it you can achieve a lot, including the making of videos ideal for social media.

If you are a microsoft and you may want to take out an online office subscription where you can download Word, Excel and other tools, although in most cases, Google Docs is an outstanding and free, viable alternative.

Lastly, depending on your industry, you may have to buy a specific set of tools to suit you. However, most online business opportunities require you to go online and use their tools, most of which are supplied for free, to encourage you to stay with them and to use their system, so in turn, you will sell through them, and normally they take a commission on anything you sell.

Before you start

Consider who your audience is, who you want to work with, time spent deciding who could save a lot of trouble and time later on.

This is so fundamental. Many spend time wondering what they will sell and promote online or offline. Instead, think about who. As a result, a much wider range of opportunities will open up for you. For example, when you have decided on who you want to work with, which may be based on those that you know, yet just as equally on those that you don't yet know, you end up with a much wider opportunity because you can go talk to them and find out what they want.

The alternative is quite a dead end in most cases and leads to many failures. That is to decide you want to sell a certain product or service and then try and sell it. If you knock on someone's door, express little interest in them, other than the normal pleasantries, you will find yourself stuck in when you get to finally tell them what you have to offer and they don't want it.

When you have decided on who you would like as your customers, you can find out where they go, what they read, why they do what they do and then, in turn, establish what they need to get done so that they cannot get done easily. Because you develop inside knowledge and learn how to address the needs, you can take what you learn for someone and offer it to others, or again start an enquiry about what they want and end up with a bunch of related services, related in terms of the industry of your customers. Your chances of making sales are enhanced.

By way of demonstration, it is important for me to encourage the self-employed, I am self-employed. They are the group of people I want to work with, particularly those in the UK, US and Europe.

Having been self employed for my whole working career, there is a lot to share, which has been my consistent passion. There is no need to go looking for people to sell my services to, these books and others like this send them to me. This book (and others) drive an online business. The book has value and its structure, so whether a potential entrepreneur comes to me or not does not matter, the book provides genuine, quality information a reader can use and benefit from as it is packed full of useful information, it is a genuine resource in it's own right. Plus, it was fun to write.

Starting your first business

The reality is you had better choose a business you enjoy, as there will be tough times ahead, days when things do not go your way (as well as days that will be brilliant), and for those down days you will need all the positive enthusiasm you can muster to bring you through.

In addition, a business is not one thing, it has to be a collection of income streams. When one slows down, the cash flow needs to continue regardless, bills still need to be paid. Ambition requires cash. Most people outgoings rise was their income rises, this is great when income is rising. However, there are such things as economic cycles and these are often caused by events outside of your control. War, political change, new taxation policies, and so on. One constant is change. So the more unrelated income streams you have, the more protected you will be.

After a while, the focus in business changes to cash management and you have to decide what to do with the cash you generate. It is a good problem to have, although it is easy to mess up, as most of us, in truth, have little experience of it.

It is super easy to spend big money on big luxuries and afterwards to have nothing to show for it, like taking the vacation of a lifetime. Or buying a big, big, expensive car. They quickly pass their sell-by date and are consigned to the past.

Multiple income streams provide better cashflow, and more profits. This means you are less reliant on one thing and ultimately more secure. Especially if each income stream is independent. So if one market fails, you have others to maintain the pace. These are insurance policies with no premium to pay, they pay you. It's great. Having said that, it is not easy, just like any other business. The point is to keep your eyes open and try to diversify to provide protection.

A recurring issue I have found is the reliance on a single party. For example, my first business was to provide a better keyboard for the Sinclair ZX Spectrum home computer, this was great while the home computer was a fashionable item. After a few years, the PC was launched by IBM and the competition was dedicated to console games machines, which became much more popular, leaving the ZX Spectrum, along with others, stranded and over a year or two, the market dwindled. I was able to move into the console market to some extent, but never to lead it as I had with my keyboard product.

The one repeated message I heard time and again: I was young enough to recover. The phrase rang true. Although really there was nothing to recover from, it was a case of simply moving on, and it was tough. What is next is a big open question not always easy to answer. I concluded, after a few years, it was about looking for a market, an audience, rather than a specific product to sell. In particular, to choose a group of people you would like to work with, where you are likely to have the most fun.

Book the business

One glance at Amazon and there are many ways you can describe it, but the one thing everyone knows is that it has the largest collection of books available through its' super fast website.

Indeed, with its invention of Amazon Prime, it also has a very high penetration among western hemisphere householders. You can sell books through Amazon for sure. You can write a book on any subject and do so without spending any big bucks.

The next thing about Amazon is that you can use the search bar to find an opportunity. So, for instance, if you choose an audience, lets say authors, you might think you could help others to write and so you can search for writers.

When you run a business, you provide a product or service that solves a problem for customers. So what problems would the authors have?

When you type in writer into the Amazon search bar, you might find an opportunity immediately. I found the term 'Writers Block', When you take a look at the results, there is some strong competition with only a few having the term 'Writers Block' in the title.

Readers choose titles that address problems with how a book looks and a big part of how a book looks is its' title. I would think it would be possible to produce a great book for that niche.

If you do some research, and come up with your own insights, and you could write an essay a day for 20 days or a little less, the chances are you will have enough content for a decent book. Most of us will be unable to write at this rate at first, however, the sooner you start, the more you write, the better your writing will become.

Every book you write, once written, is one and done, apart from the ongoing marketing and promotion required. However, if you develop a range of books on a given niche, as this author has done, for example, then the marketing activity promotes not one book, but several and each of the formats.

You can publish a book as an ebook, a paperback, a hard back and an audio book. You can then promote through more than one distributor and so one piece of writing becomes 10 saleable items quite quickly when you consider the various forms and different routes to market.

But wait, there's more. You can write a walk through the how-to course. I publish mine and give them away for free on my website, [TheAuthorityFigure.com](http://theauthorityfigure.com/) as it is all part of marketing, it increases good will, increases engagement, provides more engagement, encourages feedback and encourages me to write more books on the related topic. Thus, building an empire. Hoohahaha!

Try not get stuck in the groove of the term 'Writers Block' I am sure more than one reader of this book will think this would be a worthwhile subject. The issue here is one of competition. You really want to keep looking and find a term that is both popular and has far less competition.

You can probably tell I like the book business. I resisted it for a long time. It did seem like too much effort to me. I did not think I would have enough content. However, I did invest in writing. I bought books and I attended courses, watched YouTube videos and read other books, particularly novels. It was fun, and I started writing.

My first book was with a partner, it took ages, about three months. The next book took about three months (and needed rewriting many times over two years) although the first version was published and thanks to electronic publishing, I simply republished a new version every few months. I have edited each chapter, one a month.

The next book, and subsequent books take a few hours per day and an initial draft of 30,000 words can be done in 3 to 4 weeks, including research. I outsource cover design. I do the layout and uploaded it myself, which takes another week.

When you practice writing books, it becomes a lot easier to write an online course.

Online Training

A massive area, this can be quite a good area for business as there are millions willing to learn to develop a career, interest or hobby.

There are also many platforms to choose from. Either hosting your own training programs or platforms that will host your training and share the income with you. A good host will likely already have an audience and, therefore, customers, and this will mean you just need to focus on the training and you can leave the sales and marketing to them.

Admittedly, you cannot be in person with your students, so anything that might require power tools or machinery may not be ideal. Although it may be possible to help them with 1 to 1 zoom sessions either as part of the course or as an extra.

Each platform has a different set of merits. Some of the more well-known are known as a result of very low prices. Some are very low price (like $10) because they want to encourage understanding of a subject and a small fee covers costs. For instance, I can think of a few programming language and story telling courses that charge about that much (you have to look for them using your favorite search engine).

However, it should be noted the cost of delivering a training course, even one that lasts for hours and consists of multiple hours, costs very little, pennies to deliver, which means you can deliver thousands before the cost of delivery becomes an issue, so even at $10 this represents a huge return on costs.

The hosting sites are therefore looking for course creators as they are likely to have a lifetime of learning and all the hours necessary to write and record a series of training videos, which is not a casual activity. If it is your favorite subject, it could be fun.

You can add interactivity to your course in the shape of self-marking questionnaires, worksheets, downloads, calculators and spreadsheets, even apps and other software tools. In addition to lists of resources and summary guides.

A training course can lead to bigger things and is one reason to give them away. For example, it can take as much effort and energy to sell a course for $10 as it can for $1000.

However, once you have a course buyer, you can be certain of their interest and they are the kind of people who may be interested in further education, mentorship, consulting or joining your mastermind group.

Affiliate marketing

Affiliate marketing saves you from product creation and can provide an ideal passive income.

If you have ever bought a product or service and loved it, you may be surprised to learn you can support it on an ongoing basis to others and get paid a commission to everyone who buys that product through you.

The benefit to the supplier of the product or service is they only pay a commission on sales achieved and this minimise their sales costs and maximises their 'army' of sales representatives.

One of the leading purveyors of Affiliate Marketing suppliers is https://Clickbank.com where you can sign up as a promoter or vendor.

Many other vendors run their own affiliate marketing program, Amazon for one.

The best way to make this work for you is in areas you are passionate about. You may set up a YouTube, Twitter, or Facebook page where you will discuss your topic and these could feed traffic to your blog, newsletter, or website. Your social media, sites, newsletters, and email communications just have to include links to the vendors you recommend and if someone likes the offer, and makes a purchase, you earn a commission.

There are many who earn thousands per month through affiliate commission schemes.

Chapter 8: Start a service business

A modern service business can start up with little to no capital outlay, you just need to find your first client.

A modern service business does not need an office, storage or distribution, or to have a great deal of money tied up in capital.

They are all nice to have.

Admittedly, the more you have the better life can be, however, to get started you don't need them, you mainly need to be pleasantly determined.

Service business: definition

A service business provides advice or support to clients.

Your service business could provide support through the provision of a complete cleaning service where the service brings everything, staff, cleaning materials, fluids where the objective is to leave a target area clean, spic and span. Or, you may simply provide the staff.

If you provided the materials and, or the fluids, then you would have both a service and product business combined. If someone had to collect the materials and, or the fluids from you, then you would be said to provide a 100% product business as you do not include a delivery service.

A service business is not mutually exclusive from a product business and often the two are combined.

Indeed, many product businesses are expanded by adding services to them. You can start a business as a service business and a product range for your service business if you wish. This would be a great way to add extra value and some of your customers may appreciate the extra levels of service you offer.

Easy to start service businesses

The easiest service business to start is to teach what you know.

Academic or commercial how-to subjects to get people through exams or off to a different career.

However, you must target an audience very accurately to minimize rejection, as the majority of people will say they do not want to learn the subject you want to teach. Instead, you need to work out first, where the people are most likely to want to learn what you plan to teach.

The opposite of this is to talk to a prospective customer to find out their problem, offering them a solution. As a result, you will have to talk many fewer people.

For example, if I was offering a simple car cleaning service, I would only knock on doors where I could see a dirty car parked outside. I would know they had a need and they were likely to be in. No car, no pitch.

On the other hand, if I had gone to those doors and said I like moving, packing, mowing lawns and maintenance work, I am sure I would have got a lot of work from most houses.

An A-Z of service business ideas

- Academic services - home school teacher, language or music specialist, test preparation

- Animal Care - dog walking, grooming, sitting, veterinary, feeding

- Beauty & Lifestyle - Dating or life coach, hair, makeup or clothes stylist

- Business services - another very long list from Accountant to Virtual Assistant

- Car services - cleaning, servicing, repair, rental, inspection

- Elderly care services - companion, therapist, nurse

- Event services - events planner, fundraising, conference manager, photography, transport, and much more!

- Home maintenance and repair - a very long A-Z of services from Air conditioning to Wallpaper

- Legal services - for business or at home, private investigator, contract drafting

- Parental support - photography, babysitting, private teacher, party character

- Personal concierge services - shopper, tailor, runner, cleaner, driver

- Personal services - health and wellness

- Sales and marketing - another very long list from advertising to Social Media

- Technology maintenance and repair - computers to specialist equipment

- Travel and tourism - Adventure tours, travel planning, cruises, guides and accommodation

In most training markets, there is much competition. To me, competition simply demonstrates there is a market and this is good news.

The solution is to niche.

Niche your service business

The fundamental reason to niche down is to relate with your potential customers, so they can say you are the one for them.

Just by saying who you are for can provide you with a competitive advantage.

The formula is very straightforward {service} for {niche descriptor}.

For example, dentistry for busy families, we can further niche this by adding a geographic link. For example: A local dentist for families in downtown Denton, Ohio.

Let's say your expertise is in fitness and you want to be a fitness coach. Now think of your market and add that to the mix. For example, a fitness coach for busy entrepreneurs. Again, you may want to add a geographic descriptor for example, West London.

This may mean a lot of one-on-one service and you have to travel to them. All of this is chargeable. Missed appointments that you travel to are chargeable too. That may suit you. After all, your customers are likely to be able to pay good money and they are likely to genuinely have a need. You may even be able to create menus for them, recommend suppliers and create a wider fitness regime. Most importantly, they may be very good for referrals.

Alternatively, you may be a fitness coach and you want to work with pregnant mums on a pre or post natal basis, again there is likely to be a large audience, all of whom face similar needs and you should be able to introduce a wider care plan for them. Again, it is likely to be good for generating referrals. This will probably be run on a group basis at a single location.

Some businesses will need some up-front investment. For example, a cleaning business would require some form of cleaning materials and access to equipment, floor polishers.

It all depends on the service offered and the requirements and existing resources of your customer.

In many cases, most customers simply need a warm body who is experienced, willing and able to do the work, with all the equipment supplied, as this helps to ensure the customer always gets what they want.

In this example, the main service is to deliver a smart operator, so if a given or expected team player can't make it, you can supply a replacement and that replacement knows what to do.

Many service businesses are involved in logistics, which can range from muscle to brain power to carriage and delivery. There are many options and opportunities that vary almost as much, as there are different fingerprints. Demand is everywhere.

You might need to borrow or rent an office occasionally.

In most towns and cities, it is easy to pay for meeting rooms by the hour.

Availability varies according to location

Often it is possible to make arrangements to meet on site at your customers office, which can be very convenient for certain customers.

You may have service offices available, hotels, restaurants, or bars you can use.

I have found the bigger the customer spend, the higher an organization a decision is made. A high-up decision is one made by a Director or CEO. The higher the level, the increased the likelihood we will meet on their site. Many of my major clients have never been to my office or held a meeting anywhere else but on their site.

At other times, it is convenient to meet at a restaurant or bar, which can be expensive. Plus, they are not always conducive to business. So you generally need to scout for a location that can give you what you need in advance. Access to whiteboards is not always available, internet coverage can be patchy or overloaded and public bars can be loud.

However, much of the finance and insurance industry prefer to meet in bars and happily chat inside and out. It is possible in some establishments to reserve a table or a meeting room.

When a meeting room is available, you may wish to drag your own presentation kit in with you.

Working on site

However, if your service business is cleaning, decorating or protecting a client's office, and requires on-site attendance for the service to be carried out, the client needs to understand time is money and must be made aware of what is expected of them before the work is undertaken.

For example, floor space may need to be clear, power made available and for the space to generally vacated, or power tools may need to be made available or hired for the specific time of access.

It depends on the service you are providing, you may need special access or not, you may carry specialized power equipment. The key is to make arrangements and to set expectations in advance so on the day, at the appointed time, everything is as ready as it can be to avoid disappointment and to ensure satisfaction.

Generally, the expectation of a service provider is to turn up on time, to be smartly dressed, to look attentive, to behave, communicate well and to undertake the work professionally. I think a service provider should have the same expectations of a customer. Most usually, the customer and supplier are two professional groups of people who understand care must be taken to ensure costs are kept to a minimum and the time available is employed appropriately.

The gig economy

In most places, the gig economy has been on the rise, encouraged by lockdown and the increased requirement and expectation for web-based services.

Taking on gigs is an excellent way to find new freedoms and it has enabled some to earn what they want when they want to do what they enjoy the most. Indeed, most work can be done remotely nowadays, some are passive service businesses such as vending machines, while others are more active, such as remote coding, design work and virtual assistants.

There are, of course, many local services that can be offered on a per-use basis, or as a gig, for example pet or baby sitting, pet walking, pet cleaning, mobile veterinary service, food delivery for both humans and pets and more.

How to start a service business

In most cases, you are looking for gaps in the market. Either things are done badly or there is a problem that many suffer from that remains unsolved.

My recommendation is always to identify a group of customers you would like to work with. Perhaps you already know them, or, perhaps you know they exist. In both cases, you want to find out where they congregate and observe or attempt to discover what keeps them awake at night and then to see if you can offer a solution to their problem. If the problem is big enough, they will pay for it.

That is how you know you only really have a business when you have a customer, up until that point you only dream about having a business.

Chapter 9: Starting a product business

Rewards can high, as can be the risks

Running a product business is rewarding, it is all about stock management, however, the risks can be high.

I have enjoyed running product businesses. It is amazing to see stock piled high. Incredible to think you own it and even more incredible to know that what you pay for it is a fraction of what you sell it for.

The most important thing, though, in my opinion, is when you meet a customer who describes a problem and you both agree you have the solution and the product gets sold. If the product is your design, you can control distribution.

The business end is the area most inventors miss as most are determined to move on to invent the next best thing, understandably, to keep innovative ideas and creativity flowing.

Margins

So, unless you are an inventor able to be commercially aware, you probably want to stock, resell or distribute someone else's product.

It is my experience, that most of what you will sell will contain at least 25% margin for retailers and there is usually between 5%, 10% and at best 15% margin for a distributor.

However, there are always some lines you have to stock that are commodities with wafer thin margins.

As a retailer or distributor, then you will be very aware of the local competition. You will want to select a certain product range in more depth, or be known for being the place to come to for the best deal.

I would always recommend you steer clear of being the lowest price service provider, as all you will do is cut your margins and depend on selling more and more just to stand still to make the same profit.

For the same reason, I would steer away from commodity products too.

There are always certain sectors of the market, who will pay more. For example, professionals will generally pay more for a longer lasting, solid, recognisable, branded solution. There will be a smaller market for those, although the margins are likely to remain rock solid. Over time, you may suffer from the opposite problem, rather than dwindling margins, you could face dwindling customer numbers.

The solution is to determine and added value service, which could be training, insurance, support, or in most cases, the thing most valuable is access to celebrities, who may simply be the people behind the brand or the business.

The more entitlement you can build into your service, the more you will maintain margins and customer satisfaction.

Physical Constraints

You generally need a place to store and process goods and materials for processing.

You may need specialized storage and handling. You may need to pay special attention to protection against theft

Multi-level Marketing (MLM) is a great product-orientated business that is great for generating part-time, home-based business, after work, additional income streams.

For my first business, I rented a shop with a garage and used the shop as an office and fell foul of the local council planning department who dictated (reasonably) a shop must sell goods to the public. It was not obvious that I was doing that. I fixed this by creating a window display, and soon people would start turning up. I would serve them directly, and this turned out to be an unexpected pleasure for all involved.

Downsides-Theft

There is a lot of theft about when it comes to physical stock, through retail outlets and distribution, but not just product theft.

Product theft is real and common. Some staff steal, staff give 'discounts' to mates. Some form networks and collude together, so as to cover up theft by forging or destroying trails. Trusted staff members have been known to 'lose' stock in distribution and delivery.

I have experienced all of the above.

I am glad to say I have not experienced customer data loss. I can remember collecting credit card numbers and customer addresses by hand and storing them in a ledger. We stored the ledger in a safe, and even, on occasion, took it home in order to protect it. What I realise we should have done was dispose of the information once we had used it. For some reason, we felt it prudent to keep it, in case we wanted to bill the customer again. It was a long time ago and luckily, no harm was done. I have no idea what happened to that ledger!

Data when collected or managed is thought by some members of staff to be their property, as they compiled it, even though clearly it is the property of the business that paid them to collate and manage the data. This is not right. That is what some people think. As a result, when some people leave, they take 'their' data with them. Usually, a copy, sometimes in whole and deletes the original, so the former employer cannot use it anymore.

As a result, the most dangerous person in many businesses is the disgruntled employee who feels they are being forced out or terminated for bad reasons and takes it personally, their objective to put as much pain on the business as possible. Of course, this is wrong, illegal and short-sighted, yet it happens.

So it is vital that business owners are well aware of the issues and look at the business from a range of angles and protect themselves from these eventualities. The best way is to limit and reduce access. You want to arrange things for only those who need access to data and they get to have access to only the data they need at times when they only need it. Thus, your limit of loss may be a partial record rather than the whole database.

There is a lot to this topic and I have, with a colleague, written a whole book on it, you can find it on Amazon under the search term ESORMA, which stands for Enterprise Security Operations Risk Management Architecture. There you will find the key terms explained and the areas of business you should review in order to protect you, your staff, the business and its' clients.

Other downsides

Stock shortages, spoiled or expired stock, due to stock mishandling and poor storage systems all need to be avoided.

Many are practical matters and can be ironed out, but some of them repeat. For example, if you sell stock via an online outlet such as Amazon, you can ship to their warehouse direct from the manufacturer, this means you will not get to inspect the product, and it is not until it is shipped and a customer discovers a fault that a problem becomes evident.

In addition, in the case of working with distributors like Amazon, you may have to work hard to get a good listing within their online index and then sell out. This would mean, without sales, your ranking would drop as someone else who has stock will most likely take your coveted stock. Restocking takes both times and is often demanding cash flow.

At times, you might feel compelled to pay more for stock to be flown from abroad rather than being sent by truck and boat. Air transport has the speed benefit of keeping customers happy and maintains cash flow with the down side being a reduction in profit. You have to sell more to make the same amount, yet happy customers and profit are the name of the game.

Success depends on having access to enough cash and very good planning. Ideally, you want to predict your stock movement and employ the lowest possible costs of transport, storage and delivery. Logistics and cash are the keys to profitability. Time is used up, like it or not, every day.

Some solutions

There are a range of solutions and they mainly revolve around print on demand services, provided by some retail distributors.

An obvious example is Amazon, which produces paperback and hardback books on demand. In this case, the author owns the copyright and, as a result, when someone buys your book, only your book can be delivered. In the case of ebooks and Audiobooks, the files are held electronically and copies are sent or access is provided, so you retain the copyright ownership of those too. More reasons to like books.

There is an increasing array of products that are available on a print on demand basis. Stationary, mugs, T-shirts, wall-art, sheets, hoodies, engraved jewellery, posters, tote bags, stickers, backpacks, cushions, socks, towels, hats, water bottles, face masks, phone covers.

The ranges are increasing, as they tend to be premium-priced items and, therefore, are saleable for higher profits. Especially cute kids and baby products, and an increasing array of print on demand clothing and pet products.

Printed, branded office products have long been available and are still bought in large numbers by many companies who want to promote their brands.

However, printing on-demand products can be fast-paced and not every mug generates a sale. There are many online systems that allow you to create a product visualization like a mug with a certain catch phrase or image that may be used in an advertisement. The design costs nothing and can be created on demand, online, in seconds and instantly posted to an online store for display and, should someone order one, can then be turned around, manufactured and delivered on the same day basis, depending on your location and vicinity.

When product creation is this fast, it also increases competition and will lead you to spend more time dedicated to coming up with great designs and you will also need to know how to tune into the latest trends and spot new ones according to the general mood of the market.

Chapter 10: Starting a passive business

How to earn money in your sleep!

There are some activities that keep generating cash over and over and require little work on an ongoing basis.

Passive businesses are ideal to run on the side if you already have a main income as they generally take just a little time to manage and organize.

Passive businesses often run out of normal business hours 24/7.

A passive business is often a quiet way to build up an additional income stream. You can use income to either invest or help you give up your day job.

Many like the freedom of running their own business and often, a passive business not only provides freedom, but can demand very little from you.

However, the success of a passive business model still depends on the amount of effort you put in. In reality, in most cases, the more effort, the more reward.

Don't be fooled, there is always some work. For example, you may have a spare room, a spare floor or a spare building and it is suitable to be let and so you use Air BNB.

Once listed, you don't need to do much more than wait for customers to book, pay, arrive, stay and leave.

However, you do have to inspect the property afterwards. You may want to greet them on arrival. You may want to keep an eye on the place to make sure they don't have a rip-roaring party during their rental.

Last, the property will need to be cleaned, linen changed, and made presentable for your next guests. There is some work involved.

However, for many, this is considered a passive income. Just one property of the right size, in the right location can be enough to double the average salary.

This example may be out of reach if you do not already have an available property. There are many other examples covered in this chapter where you create assets for little to no cost which can also generate cash passively.

Capital intensive passive opportunities

Having a property to let is common, but capital intensive. While you may be lucky enough to have a property, it can be a difficult business to expand. Properties are fiendishly expensive, seemingly always rising in value, and the costs are likely to continue to rise. However, if you are an existing property owner, this may be exactly what you want, as not only does the property value rise, you can generate an income from it too. There are not many asset classes that achieve both.

If you have cash, you can buy shares and focus on those most likely to pay dividends. That is certainly passive, and many insurance and pension companies rely on this method. You may require specialist expertise to be successful, and you will be putting your capital at some risk. Investments do go down as well as up.

Another option is to join a peer-to-peer lending club. You will need to research one to determine if this is right for you. This is a way to help new initiatives and could result in loss or significant growth, you will need to assess each opportunity and decide accordingly.

You can also join a property consortium where a group club their funds together and back an investment in order to share in the ultimate proceeds.

You can save your money in a high-yield bank account, except these are few and far between nowadays, although they are generally quite safe when it comes to capital preservation.

Another option is to invest in an existing business or buy one outright, especially an online business. There are many vendors, and they can generally show years of success and growth. You can choose an online business and one that has assets, too.

For example, many authors sell the rights to a collection of their books, their associated social media accounts and connected websites on the basis that they regularly produce sales and are likely to continue for the foreseeable future.

The gamble when buying any business is usually down to whether sales will continue for beyond three years, as most deals are based on three times current profits. You may be able to see a deal where within three years you can get your money back and make a return on investment. This is likely to be the case if you are able to add a business to an existing portfolio and find synergies to reduce the cost base and release further profits.

Low cost, passive opportunities

There are many low-cost assets you can rent or buy, and indeed there are many more you can create.

A passive business based on an asset you can rent or buy could be a vending machine or some form of equipment you can rent. In the case of a vending machine, your main job will be to keep it full, so it can continue to dispense goodies. Often, in the case of renting out equipment, like tool hire, you stock it, and when needed, someone comes along and rents it. You just need to provide storage, a pick up point and to make sure it works when it is returned. Equipment hire can be competitive, and it can also be very lucrative.

Vending machines come into their own, when you have a number of them. A vending machine does not have to just dispense sweets, crisps and drinks, a vending machine can be a photo booth, where someone pops in to get an ID photo taken, for example.

Finally, there is the asset creation business. Some assets can be produced, given away or sold and yet you still own them. Sounds like a riddle, doesn't it? Well, the answer to this riddle is a book or anything that is written once and then either mass produced or printed on demand.

Online, there are many online outlets. They exist for mugs, T-shirts, pens, videos, books, audio books, and more. In every case, you own the copyright. Your job is to create the design and then to upload it to an online store, then when the store gets an order, the store creates the product and ships it to the customer and you will be paid a percentage of the sale.

It is quite possible to sell many items per day. In the short term, and it may take a while, you will likely be busy securing or creating a design in order to meet a hoped demand. Then, once your design has been created, you upload it and configure the platform in order to optimize its marketing to make sure the item(s) are found with their respective keywords.

The other activity is to find more vendors, publishers, or distributors and to load up their sites with your designs as well. In addition, you may find it advantageous to run a social media campaign to promote your product and drive traffic to the vendors. Needless to say, the vendors like this and often reward you for doing so, although the general benefit is you will sell more stuff.

The essence of passive business opportunities

Most passive business opportunities are related to the service industries, but you can make any business passive.

In essence, you can take any business you own. This would suggest that you either start a business or buy one. As soon as you can, you need to find someone else to run it, in essence, as I like to say, your job is to make yourself redundant.

However, for this to work, you need to keep a sharp eye on the figures to make sure the numbers add up in order to avoid staff from skimming the profits and perhaps selling the customers other things without declaring them to you.

One method is to take a business and to make it passive to be responsible for winning the business, then to distribute the business amongst others who will do it for less, in effect, you will be sharing the proceeds with them and you can choose to let them know this or not.

Semi-passive opportunities

This is where you deliver the first edition live and then sell your creation over and over, to a growing audience over time.

When you run a membership site or mastermind group, you will be creating content and delivering it to many once. Usually the first time, perhaps twice. First to introduce it and second time, to take account of feedback and to produce a more refined version that more exactly mirrors the needs of your audience. It can be a fun business to grow.

Affiliate marketing

Affiliate marketing saves you from product creation and can provide an ideal passive income.

You will find more detail on this topic at the end of Chapter 7 Starting an online business.

Chapter 11: Start-up marketing

How, why and where you should use mass and direct marketing techniques.

When it comes to marketing, there are two major considerations, mass and direct marketing, they can have big financial as well as problematic implications.

Mass marketing

Mass marketing is where you will want to educate a large number of people, usually by way of geography.

For example, worldwide or countrywide.

You can probably imagine how expensive this might be.

Also, it would be suitable for a product that was universally useful to consumers, such as food or soap.

The cost of this kind of advertising for most is prohibitive.

As a result of the costs involved, many brands try alternative methods, such as sponsorship. For example, Red Bull

Sponsorship may combine with PR stunts to attract a nation's attention to shine a light on the sponsors' products or services so they appear relevant and popular.

It is possible for upcoming and medium sized companies to sponsor industry-sized events to similar effect at much lower cost.

Although not country wide, at an industry event you may well get the attention of everyone who attends. This can be very effective and the effects can be demonstrated for months before and after an event and is a way to achieve rapid market prominence.

If event delegates are likely to either recommend or buy your services the focus of your campaign would be to give them reasons or materials to help them along. You could offer tools, buyers guides, or the ability to 'meet' the experts through webinars, zoom meetings, or live, online audio or video events.

As much as is practical you want to showcase your product, share insights learned as a result of recent installations. It may be useful to recount the reasoning behind recent changes and improvements. The list is endless, each infers the quality of the team behind the product and the service provided.

Direct marketing

Direct marketing works when you know explicitly who your audience is.

It is possible to buy lists of people with contact information, such as offices, home and email addresses.

You would select your list based on information held about them. They could be buyers of competitive or related products. They may be subscribers of an important magazine, event delegates based on compiled data from questionnaires or competitions.

There are many ways to acquire lists.

One way to build a list is to use your website and then, if your list has got to a reasonable size, there are services around who can take your list, build a user profile of who they think is on your list and then look for people who share similar characteristics on other lists.

List building is not usually a fast process. However, list buying can be.

There are some companies who will rent you their list, or part of it, so you can invest in a small proportion and run a test campaign.

Your objective is to send a letter or email and seek a response. When someone responds, the data is yours to use as often as you wish, you now own the data, and you must protect it.

Marketing, the essence

Many get confused and think they need to educate the whole world, that is not the case, you just want to identify potential buyers.

Whether you employ mass marketing or direct marketing, all you really want is customers. With both approaches, frequency is likely to work in your favor, the more your message is exposed to the market, the more response you can expect.

This means you need to create an irresistible offer designed specifically for your target audience to respond to.

An irresistible offer is an offer where your prospective customer would feel a fool not responding. You want your audience to feel failure if they fail to respond to you offer, you want them to feel like they are missing out.

It is vital to craft an offer that is most likely to attract the most enquiries without bankrupting you. Your offer must be in context of the service you offer.

A commonly successful offer is the humble how-to guide.

You can increase the desirability of a how-to guide by suggesting there is content you would be a fool to ignore. You could highlight this with a stand out title such as 'Six ways to increase ...' It does not have to be six, it could be another number, numbers add specificity and intrigue. What are those six ways?

You will only find out if you register for the guide.

Mass marketing tools
-Advertising (print, TV, Radio and online)

-Sponsorship

-Press and public relations

-Social Media: TikTok, YouTube, Twitter, Podcasts

Direct marketing tools
-Email marketing & follow-up campaigns

-Twitter & other social media direct messaging

-Newsletters (in print and online)

-Direct mail (print through the post)

-Referral processes and events

-Text messaging

You may be surprised to hear paid for newsletters thrive, especially when they are printed and arrive through the post, as they often become collectors' items loved by passionate followers beloved by business owners and hobbyists.

Direct mail is also surprisingly effective, probably for two reasons, first it puts information into the hands of audiences and second, it arrives in isolation and has to be thought about to be processed either to the bin, for storage or responded to.

What to communicate

With new media available at your fingertips, many are left with the question of what to communicate.

Many seem happy to share smiling faces. Happy smiling faces may help others feel good about you, your brand and your business, and is probably a good thing.

However, as a business owner and service operator, I know most companies, when it comes to paying for advertising, are looking for bottom line, business growth. Smiling faces and happy emojis rarely deliver actual, measurable, bankable sales.

Having spent millions, keyword-oriented campaigns focused on problem solving make sales. Sometimes a straightforward message, repeated over and over again, is all you need.

Share awesome information

I just can't tell you how important it is to share awesome information.

My template is straightforward. I will write a book first.

To write a book, I note down a series of bullet points. I am looking for an appealing angle, to encapsulate a viewpoint that appears missing others might benefit from.

Then, it is time to research materials on the subject. Some will be agreeable. Some materials are no more than an expanded blog post (there is that much content!). Or you will likely find key information is simply missing.

To realize information is missing is fantastic, as I found with How to start a business without any money'. A competitive title had already been published by Penguin and was written by a journalist, with no experience of running a business.

Her book contains a lot of very odd and outdated thinking, clearly written by someone trying to fill a brief. It is, I concede, probably better written than my book, after all, the author is a writer, whereas I am a business person.

The big piece that is missing from most business books is the piece about risk and what those risks might be and how to avoid them. As a business person, I spend most of my time avoiding risk and minimizing negative impact, as these things can spin out of control and bring you down, fast.

Take away the risk, and you increase your chances of success dramatically. It is not just your risk, or personal risk, you want to eliminate as many risks for your potential customers. The main thing is to adapt to potential customer needs and change what you do to suit your customers before someone else does what you should be doing. This is a strategy that will ensure you avoid getting wiped out.

Bear in mind, most end up in businesses they did not plan for. To paraphrase, the business plan, once put into action, usually falls apart on the battlefield when you discover what you really need to do in order to win and make gains.

You may have enthusiasm for a subject and you may not want to write a book or know where the missing information is. I did not want to write books. Research led to note taking and during the review process questions arose that appeared to go unanswered

Now, to write a post or a thread or write a newsletter, my books contain topics worth repeating. A simple flip to a random page of a book can locate a great idea. It is possible to refer to specific pages in your posts if you want to attribute the source - and why wouldn't you? It shows you are a well read student of your favourite subject. The kind of person most customers would like to work with is someone who is aware of current trends and is actively aware and participating.

If you had written a book, you would be taking the next step and not just observing and participating, but you would be contributing and opening yourself up, apparently for scrutiny. The reality is you would learn even more from feedback.

Simple research can speed things up and help you to organize your thoughts and information. It is part of your personal development and you will find you will build a personal repository of information that will inextricably lead you on the path of discovery to learn more about what you thought you already know.

Writing a book, to organize concepts and ideas, is therapeutic as well as insightful and has a lot more value than you might expect to you and your potential customers.

Ian Livingstone of Games Workshop suggest in Dice Men that his knowledge turned into a £2bn empire. He adapted to customer needs, under promised, and wrote things down as he went along.

Here is a recent Twitter thread I posted @TribalIdeas

Sharing is good for business

How to generate interest by giving away free information

Free information is welcomed and often shared

It is a viral way to find interested prospects

Want your business to go viral?

Read some of my top tips

Don't give your whole service away for free

Be careful about what you offer for free

The first hour free is fine

Free information is fine

The best thing to give away is a method to solve a problem

Free information solves how to get customers for free

It can be a guide, a poster, a video, or audio

Best to offer free information in all media

Consumers consume in their own way

You can provide free information on a one-off or regular basis
Become a valuable resource by sharing information regularly
Case studies, insights, industry stats, and did you know?
Updates can likewise be delivered on a range of media

Write once, publish many times
Soon, you will develop an ongoing content strategy
You will become known as the go-to resource
This will help you write new books
To add to your catalog

Chapter 12: Buying into an existing business

How to safely buy you way into a business.

Buying into a business usually requires a cash investment yet it could lead to more upsides than downsides.

There are two ways you can achieve this, one is to invest in cash where you acquire a shareholding, the other is to buy a licence.

Buying into a business through the purchase of shares generally has the dual effect of transferring share ownership to the investor and for the invested funds to be spent within the business, providing a cash flow boost for the business, which is often the reason for a company being willing to sell shares.

The benefit of selling shares can be more that the cash invested. A sales also serves to verify value, as a result of the sale. In addition, the business now has the vested interest of the investor which could bring with it other aligned benefits such as access to more customers or distribution channels.

A license allows you to operate an existing business usually in a different geographical area to the original. For example a McDonalds restaurant. The term license and franchise is generally interchangeable, there are some legal differences depending on where you are in the world.

A franchise or license generally means you will operate a business according to a set of rules.

Don't duplicate an existing brand

You could review a franchise, see it is a model that works and create your own similar business.

You could run a burger joint but you could not call it McDonalds even if your real name was McDonald. You would be sued for passing off.

On the other hand, you could set up a Fried Chicken shop and probably get away with reference to Kentucky or 'Southern Fried' and even get away with the use of a picture of a happy older man with a star-spangled hat, as many have.

However, I would suggest you take a business you like and make it yours.

The objective is to stand out and set yourself apart as unique, special, more than simply better, or worse, the best. The problem is that anything other than unique and special encourages comparison and this then brings on competition and deflates your brand equity making success and even survival unnecessarily harder than it needs to be.

Why would you want to be seen and perhaps caught out at some future date as a copycat, an also ran?

Also, differentiating from the outset is likely to save you from legal troubles and carve space between you and alternative service providers.

You may well get off to a faster start if you look like an established brand.

Yet if you do look like another business, you could find yourself getting into trouble for attempting to pass your business off as being associated with that brand or company.

If the claimant was successful, the result could be devastatingly expensive and bad for your reputation. If you are not careful, you could end up without a business at all.

Licensing and franchising are successful approaches

Licensing, or franchise opportunities seem to exist in every sector, increasingly you can find business events which showcase these kind of opportunities.

These are great if you have a pot of cash to invest in retirement and want more than a hobby, if you have just sold a business and are looking to start a new one and want to avoid starting from scratch, or if you just fancy having a part of a great branded business.

Some people will buy a franchise to play customer, to see how it all works and operates from the inside. This is so that, in turn, they can turn another business into a franchise.

There are some who finance a franchise in order to provide a relative with some form of self employment and associated prestige, which may well fit the families' other business interests.

There are many reasons for buying a business as a franchise.

The upside is that a license or franchise normally has a system, provides the opportunity to use existing branding, and importantly has systems, supplies and training available for you and your team, so you can be up and running in the fastest possible time, confident you are running a tried and tested formula.

There are usually few to no guarantees the franchise will work, as the business will still require hard work. The chances are the margins will be slim, so you will need to work hard to push the volume through.

However, volume is likely to be easier if you start with a known brand and the brand itself has an ongoing marketing campaign and local activity to drive customers to your doors.

Ultimately, you have to assess a franchise like any other business. Learn about the opportunities associated with all the upsides. Yet be aware of the downsides too, which are typically, effort and the ongoing part payment of profits to the licensee who sells the rights to represent the brand you have invested in.

Licence fees are typically paid on an ongoing monthly or quarterly basis. It is more likely to rise over time, than fall. The cost of the franchise or license is something else you need to be very concerned with and may be linked to profits or turnover.

You do not want to find yourself in a position, as some find themselves, as an overworked and underpaid employee who can't get out of the contractual obligation.

An interesting resource is the British Franchise Organisation www.thefba.org
There are issues.

Multi-level marketing (MLM)

MLM can be a very lucrative business, and some party plan-type businesses do survive for very long, particularly the home consumer brands.

MLM is usually considered by those looking for part-time business opportunities where the associated start-up costs are very low. This makes business opportunities very accessible.

However, MLM can lead to a problem known as 'garaging'. This is where a distributor in your downline has the cash to buy stock and does so in order to win a prize. They believe the stock will be sold later and take the risk. This works if they manage to sell the stock.

Be aware that garaging stock can lead to financial trouble through being over-confident or, as a result of those products being upgraded, replaced or superseded.

Garaging aside, party planners find ways to sell to their friends, relatives and neighbors. As a result, this can deplete their social contacts as many simply don't like to be perpetually sold to.

On the other hand, there are a good number of people who love it, love the parties, love the fun, which provides meaning and purpose as they can make a living from it, especially if the products are good.

Products can range from cookware (very common) to clothing (lingerie and more can be fun and popular), to cleaning, to food, to advisors to books.

An interesting resource is the Direct Selling Organisation www.dsa.org.uk

Again, as in all business opportunities, there are issues.

Chapter 13: Being the authority figure

Do you know where thought leaders go to get their insights?

Authority figures are generally well known, are well liked and customers are likely to levitate towards them, how do you make that happen?

In simple terms, one customer at a time.

Few are born or anointed as an authority, it is earned through your actions. The first action is to show others you can help and to introduce them to ideas you can demonstrate are straightforward, worthwhile, and working.

This means your demonstration is easy to promote and instantly desirable to your target audience. Therefore, the first thing you need to do is to identify your target audience. My target audience are those who are looking to start new businesses.

I have two reasons, the first is I know I can help them.

I have helped many, especially those who have big ideas and are willing to grow their business quickly. I find this exciting.

The second reason is it keeps me sharp and tuned in and allows me to use what I know. Again, it is fun and exciting.

In both cases, the benefits for me and my customers are real.

The slow way

Most businesspeople let their businesses build over time and they may not be conscious of the effect they are having and the opportunities they face.

Often they are against the idea of change. This for many is a world of missed opportunities. Not only that, but you may also be seen as an opportunity for someone to enter the market. They will copy you and improve on your execution to deliver a better, faster, and usually less expensive service to customers.

Allowing this to happen in your market could prove terminal.

You may as well be the change maker.

The fast way

Researching the true needs of a market and finding improvements shakes a market up and positions you as a game-changer, which can bring about rapid commercial success.

This is a classic approach of some fast-moving, innovative companies who are happy to state their ability to deliver game-changing results to an industry.

Demonstrating success

The ability to demonstrate success is one of the areas often underplayed and allows a new entrant to become a major competitor.

Established firms are likely to laugh initially, as new market entrants show established processes as being 'new'. Yet they are at least showing what they have and there will be many in the market who have not seen this before and so, yes, to them, it will be new.

Remember, a new entrant has no intention of selling to a competitor or peer, they are looking to carve out new markets. Every year there are new people taking on employment for the first time, or last year's intake is being promoted who will be making next year's purchase decisions and they will not know what went before. They will only see what appears to be new.

My demonstration consists of the things I say on social media, on my websites and in my books. Books are the focus of my attention when it comes to promotion and those who are interested can use the Amazon 'Look Inside' feature for free and see if they like what they read and maybe buy the book and then another, or all.

From there, with a growing knowledge of what I am about and how I can help them, they can engage with me through my websites should they wish.

The entire process flows without pressure.

Embody the idea of the authority figure

Some like to refer to the authority figure process as becoming a celebrity.

However, I take issue with that, as there are many celebrities, who, nice as they may be, are a celebrity for being a celebrity. Not for anything they have done, other than they had a lucky break.

Good luck to them.

They may want PR support, special appearances, and stunt work. I can help in all those areas, although that is not my core activity.

There is more to becoming an authority figure than being a celebrity.

For example, a celebrity is probably not a business owner and probably has few ideas about being in business other than trying to get endorsement opportunities and appearance fees. These may be lucrative; they are also random and difficult to control. For some, it works out, where it does work out, they tend to be hard workers, business people.

An outcome of becoming an authority figure can include becoming a celebrity if you want to. For example, there are many authority figures who are considered celebrities in their home markets. This means they have the benefits of being a celebrity, with opportunities to endorse and make special appearances, but can also walk through an airport without the need for security and without fear of being mobbed. The best of both worlds.

The authority figure under the hood

Every active authority figure I am aware of has strong knowledge and demonstrable fixation on purpose.

Something exists that stands out to demonstrate an area of authority that causes people to levitate towards that person and it is normally a body or catalog of work.

The clue is in the word authority: author. Being an author is not necessarily a difficult thing. You can be an author without being a writer. For example, you can speak, or record an audio or video. Your audio or video does not need you to participate, it can be the voice and the images of your customers or patients. The objective is to show transformation or to describe how transformation is possible, and how some may achieve an outcome.

Another alternative is to be interviewed or 'written up' by a journalist, partner, colleague, or student who is studying your work, or a patient or customer who is delighted with how you have helped them. In business, we also write use-cases, applications and case studies that may or may not be endorsed by clients. We collect testimonials.

Any audio or video can be transcribed. These can be edited and turned into articles and redeployed as a chapter in a book or white paper.

All these different items become documented evidence of your success and serve to underpin your authority figure position.

Ongoing authority figure positioning

Authority figure positioning is a continuous process and can be built consistently, over time.

You can build your catalog of work almost without pressure, plus you will discover ongoing innovation opportunities too.

As your catalog builds out, you will have time for introspection and you may spot areas of your portfolio that are missing or can be enhanced, this can drive special projects and set you on specific missions.

In effect, over time, you will build momentum.

Yet, each item and relevant thought can be published and tested on social media for free. This way, you can gauge how it resonates with your target market. You can determine whether to stick to the course or try another idea.

Taking the first step to becoming an authority figure

The first step in becoming an authority figure is to determine who your target market is.

When you know the who, it becomes much easier to determine your what and why.

Your who, what and why are three essential elements you need to nail sooner rather than later.

You can change them, but the sooner you start testing to see if you can build resonance the better.

From a commercial perspective, sometimes to prove something, all you need is one fee-paying customer. I had fee-paying customers before I had case studies, and before I wrote books.

I soon came to realize I could have written use cases, case studies and published books without any customers to prove the market existed. To demonstrate my knowledge and potential.

Authority figure positioning is a great way to establish a long-term presence to ensure customers prefer to come to you over anyone else.

For further information visit the accompanying site:

https://TheAuthorityFigure.com

Chapter 14: Pricing Strategies

How and why upward pricing strategies are the only way to go.

Did you know many equate value to price, and will only buy something if it is expensive enough.

However, inexperienced business owners will tend to price down their product in the mistaken belief they will sell more, as a lower price is easier to sell.

The truth is that only commodity products sell on price and, unless you operate in a commodity market, you are generally at liberty to change the price. The reality is, if you find yourself operating in a commodity market, you can change the product and this in turn can affect the price.

For example, did you know there are 50 types of chicken? Some are bread for meat, others for eggs. Some are reared in specialist factory pens, others are free range or organic while others have room to roam. Each commands a different price and some would say different quality of meat, taste and safety.

In the UK, 1 billion birds are slaughtered every year. Chicken is very definitely a commodity, yet premium ranges are available. Chicken serves a wonderful example of how you can change your core product to stay in the same market and yet introduce a premium price range.

That is the trick. Don't cut your own margins in a vein attempt to sell more. It will most likely backfire and simply help you sell the same volume for slightly less, meaning you will, in all likelihood, still struggle.

On the other hand, you can introduce a premium brand and increase the price. Let's say you increased the price by 20% and 20% of your current sales became premium by volume, then you will likely grow your business by much more than just 20%. In reality, you will have to test to reliably get to the numbers. However, normally, the classic 80/20 rule (The Pareto Principle) applies and that is how we get to 20%.

Price as a downward strategy

This is much shouted about and appears popular, it is a world of deals where the only differentiator is price.

However, the issue is loyalty. If the only reason customers come to you is to save money, then you start by cutting back all you can in order to stack the product high and sell all you can. Companies have been known to change the color of their carpets to avoid carpet cleaning bills, leading to musty (and worse) in-store smells as well as the creation of dingy, dark atmospheres.

In the end, it becomes a race to the bottom, sometimes it can be a very long race, sometimes it can be short-lived, but when the end comes, it tends to be swift. A business can with deft management and an ulcer or two manage a business with small margins. However, one mistake can trigger a wipe out event.

Invariably, to achieve lower sales prices, a business would have to take on larger amounts of inventory to get the discounts, although, often real discounts are often achieved by buying stock, the last pallet, at the last minute, usually for cash.

If something is wrong with the product, guess who is left holding the baby? Cash purchases generally or eventually require funds to finance and these are chargeable back to the lender, even if the lender is the founder. Not even founders want to lend money, take risks and do so for free. Substandard products, seconds, can also be bought and sold, these lead to not entirely satisfied clients who may even feel duped and unable to return what they have bought, are likely to refuse to buy again when they realise that the bargains available are not really bargains but are substandard products.

People are happy to pay less, but still expect perfection. Don't we all!

Downward pricing is also a real problem for the service industry. You have probably heard the phrase pay peanuts, get monkeys. The less you pay, the less service you should expect, the less time an individual service provider can spend delivering service and is very likely to deliver a minimum standard of service in order to complete the task and move on to the next one.

In certain circumstances, for certain customers, for certain service areas, this is acceptable, provided it is also legal. In many cases, you may provide a legal service, but customer demands are such that for the rate of pay, the levels of service are not deliverable, unless you are prepared to put in the extra effort without pay.

There are certain times when you might be happy to work without pay. For example, as a trial service package, or advice offered on a first hour free basis, chances working for free on an ongoing basis is not sustainable and can again lead to the swift demise of a business.

A growing business, and indeed a growing economy, can set up and sell itself for less than it cost, as the constant flow of new customers provides the cash flow to paper over losses. This leads to a falsely growing business, sometimes referred to as an over-trading business.

Most new businesses have difficulty calculating costs and so tend to under charge at first.

Profits and losses tend to work out over time.

Initially, you can expect to have the cost of a business run against you. It always takes longer than you expect to win customers and get the cash in, even if your customers pre-pay.

However, when you realize, you have to try to put the price up on your first customers who paid less originally, they may simply hold out and refuse to pay more, leaving you with a dilemma. You want to help, but you can't lose, or you take the hit and hope for better clients to come on board later, this can then cause you to trim the cost down and make mistakes, a common issue.

Price as an upward strategy

On the other hand, there are always some clients who look for personal or premium services and who are prepared to pay for certain qualities and to be recognized for being discerning customers.

You would be surprised, sometimes the most discerning customers are those who own and run discount stores on the other side of town!

I can tell you the story of the guy who makes two catalogs, one for real and the other for his wife. The pretty one is for his wife to show her friends, so she looks good.

The cheaper one is the one that sells.

This is often the case.

Often, non-glossy websites do better than the latest, highly branded tech.

People just want to be served, and it is our job to make it easier.

Typically, catalogs that look beautiful minimize text and focus on photographs. Whereas the ones that really sell include all the pre-sales information a buyer needs to verify in order to buy.

Websites can work well as they can cope with both making a product set look good and providing access to underlying data.

However, printed catalogs often outperform because buyers can see the full range just by flicking through or fanning a catalog. Catalogs can be shared and annotated. Not impossible, yet not so easy, or normal to do online.

Comparing downward to upward price strategies

Business owners and managers give themselves more choices when they employ an upward pricing strategy.

If you notice in a downward strategy, the only option is to reduce prices and this is generally achieved by reducing all costs to the bare minimum.

One store decided to change its flooring to a mud color to hide the dirt that shoppers brought in on their shoes. This meant that the store could now spend less on carpet cleaning, as the accumulation of dirt was less visible.

Changing the carpet color made logical sense.

Except dirt and damp smell after a while and it means the color scheme was based on a dark brown, sometimes wet looking darker brown base.

You can imagine, this does not create the best shopping experience.

On the other hand, if you focus on an upward price strategy, you can afford to spend more on service, have a better quality of carpet, pay for more regular carpet cleaning and create a far better customer experience.

This approach will not suit everybody. You may lose some customers to cheaper competitors. However, you will graduate to serving better and better clients who will spend more, buy more often and be more likely to brag about their purchase and you can help them with that too.

An additional lever you have to play is customer recognition. You can provide branded bags, proudly branded products, uniformed staff, concierge and delivery services. Especially the kind of delivery services neighbors can see. You may offer it as a labor-saving service, and you may charge for it. However, your customer wants it for another reason than to let his or her neighbors know where they are shopping. Prestige shopping is the best offer to make.

With prestige shopping, you can also offer red-rope treatment, members only services and various levels of service, blue, silver, gold, diamond, black for example, just like the colors offered by credit card companies. The primary offer is to infer prestige on the card carrier.

It may seem far-fetched, but these kinds of strategies are worth building into your start-up business just as soon as possible as they lead to the things you need when you are starting out. More income, higher prices, and most importantly for customers to come to you.

Chapter 15:
Limited liability

Incorporation,
legal, accounting,
customers
money, terms
and conditions -
administration!

Limiting liability is a big issue and reflects the risk involved in a business and how much you would be liable for if things go wrong.

Laws vary from state to state and country to country, and liability is worth finding out about. One free source of information may be an insurance broker who may be able to let you know of the minimum legal requirements you need cover for and may be able to recommend advisors. An insurance agent will try to sell you insurance. However, in the event of a claim, insurance could be a wise investment and may prove to be an inexpensive cost.

Certainly, most of my needs are covered with a very small monthly payment. Plus, it provides me with access to free legal advice that has helped dodge the bullet on one of two false issues.

Incorporation

Incorporation is a definite cost and is often incurred before you have any business, usually because you think it is important to be incorporated.

Limiting liability is important. This is a function of risk and can only occur if you make a sale and does not necessarily stop anyone from suing you personally if you have provided what they think is advice.

Many people get carried away with this and think for months about the most appropriate name, where to incorporate, tax domiciles and so on. I am not sure it makes much difference, not at first. I would recommend that the first thing you do if you are concerned is get some insurance to provide actual cover against liability. The rest of it just takes time and only really matters once you make a lot of money. If you start making real money, the incorporation and advice services are bountiful, available everywhere. There are many who will only be happy to provide advice.

When I incorporated, I bought a company off the shelf and chose one with a meaningless name.

I chose one called Herman Reeds Ltd, it meant nothing, yet sounded professional and it turned out clients loved it. I have never met anyone called Herman in my life.

Another company, my second, was Alterindex Ltd, that inextricably turned out to be an SQL term (systems terminology for a certain type of database) which was an accident, although I was involved in databases and it turned out to be appropriate.

I bought that company simply because it started with an A and it meant I would be at the top of the directory. I was not thinking that way when I later bought Weboptimiser, which was a name I had thought about.

Although, as it turned out, I did not think of the US way of spelling it as weboptimizer, nevertheless, customers, especially those in the US, loved dealing with a London-based supplier. I guess it was cool.

Legal and accounting services

I worked extensively as a supplier to a high end city based accountancy and tax specialist firm, they offered no services to my kind of small business.

At that time my business was strictly in the small beer league, maybe half a million a year in income, no advertising spend commissions, just pure service fee. It was big at the time, big to me anyway.

I knew you could spend a fortune with this particular firm of accountants and when I asked them I learned a big lesson.

They politely told me they did not have any services to offer me.

A neat let out.

What they meant was obviously I could never be able to afford their rates and they would not like such a low-paying company as a client.

I get that now.

I was green and wet behind the ears when I heard it.

I was glad to hear those, words, I learned a lot from that phrase. It really struck home.

Not from the perspective that it was offensive or insulting, but from the fact that they had a clear idea of what their clients looked like and my 'liddle old' business was not a fit. A great lesson learned. As a business owner, you can't possibly serve everyone, you decide who your customer is and go after them.

I then looked for lawyers who would suit me and I found that I could get them in a service package called factoring as I detail below and through insurance that included legal support. Also, when I started hiring people, I hired a specialist employee handbook company that also provided insurance and support, which turned out to be invaluable as I employed hundreds of people over many years and all sorts of weird and wonderful situations occurred, including theft.

Hiring a set of accountants was similar. I did not take on any accountants. I looked for a firm who was able to show me they were competitive and would quite a fee that would get me through and be able to provide additional services as needed. I largely stuck with the same partner for several decades, as it kept everything clean and simple.

Customers money

I refer to using customers' money to grow a business and this is worthy of a clear definition.

First of all, you should always spend customers' money on products or projects to the benefit of the customer.

You have to be clear and careful about how you use customers' money, as it is their money. Often it is possible to ask for a deposit to be paid to allow you the opportunity to buy certain goods on their behalf. It would be a good idea to not only say this verbally, but also to confirm this in an email, to make sure there is clarity. Usually, deposits, once paid, are not refundable. You may want to state that in your terms and conditions.

Ideally, you more than likely retain some professional liability until the finished products or goods are delivered to them.

Terms and conditions

You will find you will develop several sets of terms of conditions and they will be made available to your customers and staff before an order is placed on you and will be considered as part of the order.

Generally, the law around the world (check in your jurisdiction) is that a customer has the right to choose from a variety of suppliers and when they choose you, place an order on you and that order is delivered, they have to pay whether they like it or not. Some customers do not appreciate this, and ultimately, you do not want an unhappy customer. So, most of the time, we will try to find a happy compromise, so they do get what they want and you get a clean sale.

There are situations where certain customers refuse to be happy. This may well be because their circumstances have changed and their objection is a ruse to avoid payment, for whatever reason. This is a customer who cannot be satisfied. It is naughty, but it happens.

Some customers will accept 99% of a delivery and find fault with 1% and not make any payment until the 1% is fixed. If that is reasonable and an easy fix, fair enough. Sometimes the percentages are at odds with reality, and again, this can become an unreasonable situation.

At other times, the buyer changes and the person you sold to is not the same person who now takes delivery. Again, perception issues about what was expected and what was delivered may appear.

For all these reasons, you want to set out clearly what it is you are selling, in detail, including the roles and responsibilities of each party in the transaction. The more detailed, the better. Previous deliveries, testimonials, examples, photographs and drawings can all feed into the evidence to demonstrate you have delivered the goods according to the order and that payment is now due.

Usually, a good set of terms and conditions fixes most problems.

I found that factoring my sales, also known as invoice discounting, is a very good solution. Some people look down on this, yet it can be very cost-effective. Especially if you are selling repeatable services to strong clients.

A factoring company is usually a bank. It works by having clear paperwork, overseen and approved by the bank and signed and agreed with each client. You get an order, the paperwork is completed accordingly, it is a very professional process where you explain that, for expediency, all invoices are handled by the bank. These are sales invoices.

When you have completed and delivered the order to issue an invoice to the client for the work done and pass a copy to your factor company, the bank. The invoice says the client is to pay the factor company. Invoice chasing and collection is now handed over to the factor company. This saves you, the service provider time and money and avoids sending copies of invoices, liaising with the clients' accounts department and any difficult conversations about when payment will be made that may occur in the future.

Instead, if you need money, you ask the factor company to pay an advance on the invoice and they will usually pay 70% same or next day, even before the invoice is due. You do have to pay interest on the borrowed amount, but it is small and you have the cash you need to pay wages and to grow the company without over trading or taking major risks.

An additional benefit is that you would usually pay a small premium per invoice to cover against customers not paying, if they go bust or decide to argue, or if the company has to take them to court to get payment. All that is out of your hands.

Personally, I found that this process relieved a lot of grief and saved a lot of money, especially compared to money I would have lost to non-paying clients against whom I tended not to sue. Whereas this way, it was up to the bank to sue, and it seemed clients tended to believe they would and so the whole issue went away.

The extra bonus is that customers tend to last longer and not try to pull silly tricks, just to get out of paying the last invoice. Not paying the last invoice is a common trick some customers pull on the basis they decided they would never have to deal with you again. Unfortunately, this is how business can be.

Seek profession advice first

This book is focused on concepts I have employed. These may not be something you can employ.

I refer you to the disclaimers and copyright notice on page 1 at the beginning of this book. For further clarification and before you take action on any of my experience, please seek professional advice first.

Chapter 16: Your next steps

This is the path to exponential growth

Many expect to pitch for business, pitching means you are in a commodity market.

You are doing something seriously wrong if you are invited to pitch. It may mean a client has a policy of never buying anything unless a range of suppliers have been seen. This is a process which clients often refer to as death by PowerPoint sessions.

They can be won, I have won some. However, generally the client has already selected a supplier they would prefer and are simply going through the motions and learning other creative approaches, they can then run through their preferred supplier.

The best thing you can do is to change the description of what you do. You must avoid multi way pitches where you position yourself as a commodity that creates a downward pressure on price and ultimately a loss of market share as you become an also ran. You stay on top of the market by leading the market by definition.

Pitching may also be what you might do at an incubator when you are one of 20 and only two will get funded. You keep pitching until you get funded and you listen for feedback and modify your pitch to cover all the angles. Some will go as far as to make an explainer video that shows off what your service will be about.

When you go to see a customer, it does not work that way. You need to listen. You have two ears and one mouth. Your mouth should basically say agreeable things, and you should listen very carefully. You are being given time because the buyer believes and hopes you can do the job. If you can, it saves the buyer from finding another supplier. You must not lie, but you must be very agreeable.

Honesty really is the best policy

You should be straightforward and honest at all times.

I have attended many meetings and the potential customer has opened with a statement like 'OK, what have you got for me then?' After all I talked us into having a meeting.

Even if it is a zoom meeting.

I will often respond by saying 'I am not sure exactly, I have a lot of things I could offer, but really I want to hear from you. What do you have in mind? If you tell me I can create the best solution for you?'

Perhaps the prospect will open up and provide some clues. If it is like getting blood out of a stone, I might be happy for a while and then come back to 'you were happy to arrange this time, so I think you may have something in mind, can you tell me more about your business and the problems you have to overcome?'

Indeed, just about the whole of the first meeting, I will be asking straightforward questions to discover what the need is, when they need it done by, how many people will be involved, who will it involve, and is there any evidence I can view, or people I can meet while we are here.

The more I can engage the client in the buying process, the more information I will have to quote for and the more involved or engaged the client will be. The more engaged, the more likely that client will buy from me, for the simple reason the client would probably prefer not to go through the entire process again with someone else.

No doubt the client will have questions.

I will answer them and use them as a trail close, such as 'Is that a good answer for you?'

Essentially, if it is not a good answer, I want to know why not and either fill in the outstanding blanks, clear up any misunderstanding or explain how it could potentially be managed. I find customers like can-do suppliers.

At no point, do I say 'no can do'. Unless it is illegal, against my personal morals and ethics or I really dislike someone's approach to business.

For example, if we are talking about a 100k job spread over a year and payment will only be made in years' time, then, well, no. If it is a large job and there is a major issue with something that costs a few bucks, that will set warning bells.

Finally, agreement must be made on payment terms, and again if there is anything non-standard I will worry again.

For example, I will not do cash deals in carrier bags or travelling cases or much in the way of barter.

Perhaps I am missing out. However, I have heard of a number of people getting caught out for playing those kinds of games.

Is the business sustainable?

The next step, once you have found a business, and you have your first client, you need to make sure the business is sustainable.

In simple terms, this means you need to sell more to your existing customer and you need to seek new, additional customers.

You can achieve success in several ways.

You can seek repeated orders by increasing the volume, or the repeat frequency. Perhaps you can influence consumption so your customer needs to buy more and you put the price up.

Many will baulk at the idea of putting the price up.

Surely, the objective is to sell more and put the price down as an incentive. Maybe, perhaps.

However, once you have completed a job, only then do you know its' true cost, so take a moment to evaluate. You have probably charged too little.

When you first quote for work, you may as well tell your perspective client this is highly likely to low a price. Ask them to review the price and to give you feedback, the question: have you charged enough in their opinion to do the job. They will rarely suggest you charge more, they are more likely to say something like, if you bring that in on time and I like it, I will pay you 10% more.

However, I have heard some clients tell me that parts of my quote looks light for what they have in mind and so this is required fine tuning, that may well increase the price.

Getting the price right is important, remember they have largely decided they want to do business with you.

My general experience is the first sale is typically undersold in two ways.

First, the price is too low compared to the value delivered.

This varies according to experience and how timid you are. I am always annoyed when a customer bites my hand off when I sell something as I immediately know I sold it for a price that was too low.

Secondly, a low price can indicate low value.

Discerning customers are afraid of paying too little and would rather pay more to get good quality.

A higher price is not a rip-off.

We can always sell things for less.

As you will know, the less you pay, the less you will receive.

Quality in all areas of experience tends to go down, not up.

So if you are buying a car to ferry your family around, do you want a weak, underpowered car that could get you into scrapes compared to a strong, protected, powerful nippy car that can ensure you zoom out of them safely?

Add value to avoid discounts

Essentially, after your first sale, you may understand more about what you were expected to put into what you sold and you may conclude it was a great experience, but for you, just not particularly worthwhile financially.

You don't want to become a busy fool. You have to put your price up to make sure you get paid properly, this is 100% on you and your decision. It is an opportunity to give yourself a pay rise and if the customer is delighted, then so should you be.

The temptation is to offer a lower price, a quantity discount. Just bear in mind your customer will still only buy the numbers they need, so the margin of discount is the margin you have decided to lose.

Add value instead.

If you buy these three, you get this valuable, wonderful bonus. Sometimes, the free bonus can be more valuable to your customer than the core product. Often the bonus is nothing more than recognition, like a prize, or to be featured as this month's best customer, or feature in some form of joint promotion is an even better option and opportunity as you both benefit from cross endorsement.

Exponential growth

Find more customers.

This can be a problem if you have not already put in the work to determine who your customers will be. See the Authority Figure chapter.

You need to determine early on who you are for. This is a topic I cover more via the accompanying books website, https:// TheAuthorityFigure.com and the 'How to Wow' free training offers.

When you know who your customer is, you can get clear on what they want, you will know where they are, how to contact them, what keeps them awake at night, the offer most likely to deliver results and what to say to them when they become an enquiry so you can turn them into customers.

If you take the price and increase it by just 10% and you double your customer base from 1 to 2 and you increase the frequency of sales from say, just once a year to twice, which is enormous double-digit growth.

The more ways you can find to double your customer growth, double repeats, and double the price, the more sustainable and solidly reliable your business becomes. Indeed, you will experience exponential growth.

Thank you

Make sure you register on the books accompanying website at https://TheAuthorityFigure.com/ to ensure you acquire more insights into how to start your business.

You will also receive the most recent updates and access to a range of bonus materials, videos and resources as discussed in this book. You will in addition receive updates by email on other books in this series.

In conclusion, thank you for reading this book. I hope you have as much fun running your business as I have had running mine.

If this topic interests you, make sure to sign up for my free newsletter https://theauthorityfigure.substack.com/ where I have more to share.

Would you please leave a review on Amazon. Thank you. Reviews help other readers find the book. You would provide a great service to this author and future readers.

www.ingramcontent.com/pod-product-compliance
Lightning Source LLC
Chambersburg PA
CBHW050643190326
41458CB00008B/2405